Living Beyond the Nation

Tea Golob

Living Beyond the Nation
European Transnational Social Fields and Identifications

Bibliographic Information published by the Deutsche Nationalbibliothek
The Deutsche Nationalbibliothek lists this publication in the Deutsche Nationalbibliografie; detailed bibliographic data is available in the internet at http://dnb.d-nb.de.

Library of Congress Cataloging-in-Publication Data

Names: Golob, Tea, author.
Title: Living beyond the nation European transnational social fields and identifications / Tea Golob.
Description: 1 Edition. | New York : Peter Lang, 2016. | Includes bibliographical references and index.
Identifiers: LCCN 2016016579 | ISBN 9783631678664
Subjects: LCSH: Group identity--Europe. | Nationalism--Europe. | Transnationalism.
Classification: LCC HN373.5 G65 2016 | DDC 361.6/1094--dc23 LC record available at https://lccn.loc.gov/2016016579

ISBN 978-3-631-67866-4 (Print)
E-ISBN 978-3-653-06984-6 (E-Book)
DOI 10.3726/978-3-653-06984-6

© Peter Lang GmbH
Internationaler Verlag der Wissenschaften
Frankfurt am Main 2016
All rights reserved.
Peter Lang Edition is an Imprint of Peter Lang GmbH.

Peter Lang – Frankfurt am Main · Bern · Bruxelles · New York · Oxford · Warszawa · Wien

All parts of this publication are protected by copyright. Any utilisation outside the strict limits of the copyright law, without the permission of the publisher, is forbidden and liable to prosecution. This applies in particular to reproductions, translations, microfilming, and storage and processing in electronic retrieval systems.

This publication has been peer reviewed.

www.peterlang.com

Acknowledgment

The research presented in this book was undertaken as a part of my doctoral research fellowship funded by the Slovenian Research Agency. This fellowship was hosted by the School of Advanced Social Studies in Nova Gorica (Slovenia) from 2010 to 2015. I would like to thank my friends and colleagues there for their support and especially their willingness to help me establish contacts with my interlocutors in the European Commission. My research interest for transnational processes and identifications goes back to my MA studies, which I carried out under the European joint programme (CREOLE) conducted by the University of Maynooth (Ireland) and the University of Ljubljana (Slovenia), and it still continues with my post-doc studies at the School of Advanced Social Studies in Nova Gorica. The relationship between personal evaluations and social context placed in the transnational social reality is still a part of my present reconsiderations of the theoretical perspectives and empirical explorations of various European social fields, as for instance the field of European education.

Table of Contents

1. Introduction 9
2. Contemporary social order and identifications 17
3. Transnational social fields 21
4. European social fields 35
   4.1. Towards the insights from the field 50
5. European bureaucratic social fields 55
   5.1. Fieldwork and analysis of ethnographic material 57
   5.2. Putting flesh on the bones 58
      5.2.1. Predispositions influencing the entrance to the transnational social sphere 59
      5.2.2. Transnational social forces 62
      5.2.3. National social forces 65
      5.2.4. Intersubjective meaning 68
      5.2.5. Instrumentality and strategic action 70
6. Conclusion 77
7. List of references 83
8. Index 93

1. Introduction

The common thread of this book reflects interests in the processes of identification linked to transnational social spheres. It elucidates the fact that transnational layers of identification are instrumental and result from strategic deliberations. The ability to add a transnational component to other layers of identity signifies reflexive individuals who are more capable to recognise enablements and constraints of an ever more complex and differentiated society than those wedded solely to national social context. Social spheres, be they national or transnational, are perceived as social environments in a broader sense, not limited to physical spaces or communities, but pertaining to socially constructed or imagined spaces. With increasing complexity of the social systems, individuals have begun to enter a variety of social environments and were confronted with the multiple meanings of social order. Semantics offered by social environment trigger individuals to actively respond to a social context. However, we do not just intend to discuss contemporary transnational identifications in general, but to put flesh on the bones as well. we further deploy the theoretical assumptions in regard to possibilities for empirical implications, which call for the consideration of social fields, particularly the European ones. The book draws its insights from the in-depth interviews with civil servants working in different departments and services of the European Commission, who are participating in the transnational social field of the Eurocracy. Their identifications reflect a complex geometry of definition of a self within a variety of social, political and cultural contexts. The main goal is not just to illustrate different layers of identities ranging from local and national to European ones, but to represent that these identifications are indeed instrumental and strategic. We reveal that interlocutors are capable of revaluating their position inside the social structure and of orienting their actions towards better life opportunities. They are able to cross national boundaries and to strategically create new lives in transnational social spheres. They cannot escape social constraints though their deliberate and strategic actions turn constraints into enablements offered by the social environment.

The introductory chapter is therefore the venture point to a brief, yet comprehensive, presentation of theoretical framework and its potential for empirical implications regarding contemporary identification processes, which are torn between local, national, transnational or even supranational social spheres. The theoretical basis for exploring the overlapping referential frames of structural semantics substantiating recognition of selves and others is set in the context of transnational social fields. They enable exploration of identifications that emerge as a result of individual experiences within different national communities or groups, institutional rules and transnational connections.

In order to dig into a complex interlacing of intimate evaluations and social determinants underpinning the comprehensive process of defining a self, two concepts are deployed: reflexivity and habitus. A simultaneous consideration of both conceptual notions within a context of individual or collective biography broke academic ground more than a decade ago, in an attempt to incorporate Bourdieu's ideas into a contemporary, individualised and unstable social reality (cf. Adams 2006; Mouzelis 2007). Due to various ontological dilemmas that see the human subject or consciousness on different levels, emphasising epistemic relativity of phenomenological perspectives, as does Husserl's philosophy, or as a real substance, as does Bhaskar's critical realism, the combination of both concepts has become quite a burning issue (Archer 2010; Caetano 2014; Akram and Hogan 2015). In this book, we incorporate both concepts into an analytical framework of contemporary identifications as a useful theoretical and empirical tool. We don't attempt to hybridize both concepts (cf. Adams 2006), but to show what changes the transformations of the social order have brought, which demand intensified consideration of reflexive deliberations. At the same time, this should not be perceived as "imperative of modernity" (Archer 2012). Although individuals are not confronted with the static social structures typical for pre-modern conditions, they do depend significantly on a structural context, which can trigger or obstruct reflexive deliberations.

Human beings and social order are seen as two emergent entities, which cannot directly influence each other. There is no structural determination directly influencing individual subjectivity, and vice versa. Human beings are environments to each other and to social systems, which are positioned towards each other as they are towards human beings. The relationship between them can occur only in terms of structural coupling, which has been well explained by Luhmann (1999). All systems, not to forget physical systems, as are our body or brains, are emergent units, which are autopoetic. Human beings are presenting an environment to social systems in terms of their consciousness or their inner space of mind. They are reproducing and maintaining their existence via an on-going process of self-description, that relies on the information stored in their brain to compile the information offered by a social environment. As Luhmann (1995) asserts, self-description or operational mode of consciousness is not a deliberate process by default that is actually quite rare. We cannot intentionally follow all the thoughts and actions that we produce in our environment. The compilation of information disposed to particular consciousness depends on the operational processes of someone's brain - information stored can be understood as memory - and on the social positioning of the individuals exposing them to particular semantics of social order, offered by social environment. Furthermore, the operational mode of each consciousness is, due to its own emergent properties and auto-poetics of reproduction, unique. This makes someone's identifications simultaneously personal and collective, as social embeddedness designates a shared experience, which, in sociology, is called a field, a social group, a social class etc.

The collective repertoire of available semantics offered by a social environment shared by humans, who are similarly embedded into the social context, can be understood as habitus. In Bourdieu's (1990) sense, habitus is a schema of dispositions that impose structure of the field and orient routine actions. Habitus is therefore imprinted social structure in form of cognitive dispositions, which entails the subjective framework for actions. As Adams (2006, p. 515) says, there is a place for individual agency but in terms of pre-reflective orientation. Bourdieu did recognise the role of reflexivity, but considered it as much the habitual outcome of "field requirements as any other disposition". Here, the habitus is seen as an intertwinement of different social and cultural information that can, but doesn't have to impinge, upon individuals' actions. That information can represent a repertoire of unconscious dispositions, which orient routine action or can become a conscious repertoire of choices leading to deliberation and actions. The confrontation between a social context and individual projects plays an important role here.

The mutual influence between social structure and human consciousness is an inter-reaction between causal powers of both emergent properties. The important role is played by "trigger-causality" (Luhman 1995, Seidl 2004), meaning that human consciousness is a trigger to social systems whose structures respond in their own specific way of reproduction, and vice versa. Social embeddedness of individuals reflects the variety of social environments, which they can potentially trigger. The structural coupling between social systems and human consciousness is made by confrontation between communication, which is an emergent property of the social systems, and thoughts, that are emergent properties of individuals. One of the personal emergent properties of consciousness, which leads to morphogenesis, is reflexivity (cf. Archer 2003).

When conceptualising reflexivity, we lean much on Archer's (1988) perspectives, as she argues for analytical dualism and rejects the conflation between structure and agency. She strongly criticizes the idea of structure and agency to present two sides of the same coin, as Giddens proposed. She argues that the particular mode of reflexivity to emerge and become a subject's personal property refers to a nexus between a context contributed by the socio-cultural structure, and concerns contributed by active agents.

Reflexivity is not just a reflection referring to self-transcendence, therefore being capable to observe oneself as an object. Through the processes of discerning, deliberating and dedicating (cf. Archer 2007) it leads to concrete deliberate actions and not just to (self)-perceptions. The observation of 'I' through 'Me' is a trademark of the Meadean tradition (Mead 1934) and is maintained by the symbolic interactionist and pragmatist tradition (James 1890; Peirce 1958). Following Archer, we advance those considerations. Reflexivity is not a generic mode of self-observation, as it was already proposed (cf. Porpora and Shumar 2010), but due to unique internal conversations produced by consciousness, it takes a variety of forms.

On the basis of reflexivity, individuals adopt certain "stances" towards society, which constitute the micro-macro link and produce the "active agent" (Archer 2003; 2007). Having a personal identity, as defined by their individual configuration of concerns, they are able to decide what they care about most and what they seek to realise in society (Archer 2003). In that light, reflexivity is a key mechanism for social change, taking shape through the relationship between individual and structure, but always in the domain of individuals (Archer, 2003). Individuals reflexively influence their actions; by so doing, they simultaneously influence the social structure. In that sense, reflexivity is a mediator between structure and agency.

However, we have some doubts about Archer's (2012) rejection of the existence of habitual action or habitus in the late modern era. In her recent views, late modernity induces the strong role of reflexivity which had brought her considerations closer to overwhelming reflexive capacities permeating all aspects of social life. She also strongly disagrees with any attempts to combine both concepts as a conceptual tool. We believe that the consideration of both concepts in exploring social practices and identifications can be productive, but certain amendments need to be made in that regard. Attempts to accommodate Bourdieu's habitus into late-modern social transformations directly does not seem to be productive, and it is certainly not enough just to broaden Bourdieu's definition of reflexivity. His theory of practice and reflexivity is too deterministic and obsolete; also, the concept of habitus is insufficient in that regard. It is important to take into account the instability and complexity of social order, to challenge the implicit assumptions of unreflexive individuals (Sayer 2010) and to pay attention to interactional and figurational inter-relations between actors, which condition reflexive competences (Mouzelis 2007).

Habitus can be perceived and understood as a set of dispositions that can be acquired in relation to certain social and psychical environments. Structural coupling occurs on the level of the individual and of social structure, but also between individuals, who intersubjectively absorb information from each other. As Bottero (2010, p. 20) says, when considering identity construction and action, one should take into account that individuals share their perceptions and beliefs, and continually provide "accountability" to each other as a basis of coordination of understandings and practice. Although those dispositions can be unconscious, they are in no way deterministic. In certain social contexts, they can become reflexively evaluated, and lead to a conscious social action.

The combination of both these concepts can indeed be very productive, however, the ontological nature of reflexivity, having an autonomous role in mediating structural and cultural conditioning, has to be maintained (cf. Mrozowicki 2010). Habitus is thus a puzzle of different dispositions, gained in different life stages according to participation in particular social environments or fields. Each part of the puzzle is activated in different social contexts and can operate as a source for reflexive deliberation or as an unconscious dimension of consciousness.

Due to the instability of social order and overlapping social environments, in which one participates, we can differentiate between primarily ascribed components of habitus gained by birth and primary socialization and secondary ascribed components gained throughlife. In traditional social order, primary components dominated, as movement between social fields was not common. The contemporary social order has produced social contexts, which encourage the reflexive deliberation of perceptions, valuations and thoughts more regularly.

As Archer (2003) says, belief, thoughts or desires are a first order of mental activity, which can fall into either the private or public domains. It can originate in a set of predispositions. What truly refers to private mental activity, which can only be conscious, is a second order activity-reflexivity in which individuals deliberate upon beliefs, thoughts or desires. Each person has her or his own private space and exercises reflexive deliberations, but there are some conditions that influence whether one can evaluate the situation in which one is embedded as enablements or constraints that act as potential causal powers of social emergent properties. The resources one has available influence whether someone is capable of moving from primary agency towards collective agency or even to the position of individual actor. It could be said that while evolving into second order of mental activity, the products of first order activity, i.e. belief, values and thoughts, can be evaluated as contested exerting personal concerns or can be accepted as such. This implies a passive agent, for whose social action dispositions do play an important role. Although Archer (2012) suggests that the reproduction of any given beliefs refers to a communicative reflexivity, one cannot see sets of social or cultural (pre)dispositions only as a substance that serves as a basis upon which internal conversation leads to reflexive deliberations. There are social and cultural contexts that can influence social action in an unconscious manner, or condition imagination of individuals. Sayer (2010, p. 121), who attempted to combine internal conversation with habitus while leaning on a vast amount of fieldwork material says that

> "without habitus, it is hard to imagine how we could ever be comfortable, competent actors, able to act partly without thinking what we are doing – or indeed able to act competently, even in social situation, while having internal conversation at the same time about something else."

We find Archer's statement that each person has her or his own inner place which cannot exist without constant inner conversation as plausible, but we do not see inner conversation as a constant deliberate activity, but more in Luhmann's terms of self-referential reproduction. Thoughts are elements of consciousness, which are replacing their predecessors in order to exist. Psychical systems have to be constantly engaged in self-description, which leads to semantics substantiating their personal and collective identities. Humans can also reflexively deliberate upon social context and thus intentionally construct instrumental identities, but we do not interfere with social context directly. Our agential powers evoke particular socially emergent properties (i.e. enablements and constraints) on which we can deliberate. If the exercise of enablements and constraints is contingent upon personal agency (Archer 2003), one needs to orient ones concern to particular social contexts in the first place. And there is a crucial role of different resources conditioning our social embeddedness or involuntary agential positions.

The lack of resources impacts someone's concerns resulting in the absence of reflexive deliberation or its particular mode. If I lack particular resources in my youth (material, social, and cultural, educational), I may not be able to recognise my position as unpleasant or may not have enough resources to orient my personal ambition into changing my position. Simplifying the complex personal situation in order to illustrate the prepositions, it could be said that if I grow up in a discouraging environment, working as a child labourer, denied any education and being raised in a belief that this is my destiny, I still have my emergent property of inner conversation. However, in monitoring myself I am not able to orient my thoughts to different social contexts, as I judge it necessary. My second order mental activity (i.e. reflexivity), if it appears, contributes to a reproduction of thoughts, beliefs and values. Therefore, I remain involved in primary agency and being relatively passive. I do not induce the enablements and constraints of structural properties. The set of structural dispositions and cultural information can be revaluated through inner conversation, but my social position, embeddedness defined by disposition, and cultural frameworks remain consistent with my personal identity acquired as a result of the first causal power of reflexive deliberation. The set of disposition or habitus thus becomes overwhelmingly relevant. As a passive agent, I am more a medium of dissemination of cultural information than social structuration. The set of my dispositions substantiates my identities. Therefore, in order to explore identities which are substantiated with rooted values and orientation, the concept of habitus represents someone's compilation of cultural information but does not consciously change them. However, the situation of late-modernity has impacted the unconscious dimensions of our behaviour significantly, and emphasised the role of reflexivity as a mediator between individual and social structure.

2. Contemporary social order and identifications

Due to social transformations that resonate with technological development, the development of mass media and global connectivity, the repertoire of social information has increasingly become a matter of choice. It has been argued that new unpredictable and uncertain social areas have emerged, which influenced a number of transitions in everyday life as reflected in the character of social organisation and in the structuring of the global system (cf. Beck, Giddens, Lash 1994). The world we live in seems to be unstable; everything appears to always be on the move. Social, economic and cultural connectivity have come to be an inevitable fact and the regular movements of people, goods and ideas have increasingly become part of everyday reality. The accelerating "time-space compression" (Harvey 1989) forms a condition for social change that expresses dynamics between agents and social structures on several global and local levels. Individuals and their position in society have come to be seen in the light of ever-changing global conditions and transnational connections.

The influence of the rapid flow of mass media images, scripts and sensations brought about "a new order of instability in the production of modern subjectivities" (Appadurai 1996, p. 6), while networks of social relations, cultures of adaptation, and political and economic institutions also work on global and transnational levels. Expansive changes in communication technologies and structures led to the relativisation of our established cultural and individual practices, while the multiplicity of ideas influences the perception of the self and identities (Gergen 1991). Identity constructions in the contemporary social order call into consideration issues such as personal intimacy, imagination and reflexivity and also their relation to the social (or cultural) contexts, which have lost their stability and predictability. The complexity of information to which one is exposed offers a wider framework for the interpretation of someone's position within a society and one's strategies that ensue from it. There cannot be identity if there are no tools, social or cultural, to interpret its substance.

The traditional approaches (Mead 1934; Erikson 1959) tackled identity as a concept referring to the continuity and stability of social structures, and emphasised fixed social role models as tools that help individuals construct their identity. Such models thus revolved around professions, social roles, performance and inherited positions in public and private spheres (cf. Kellner 1995). Alongside the growing awareness of globalisation, transnational economic, political and social currents, and the expansion of mass media, identities have become detached from fixed social places and groups.

As a result of increasing complexity of social order the reduction of meaning in the self-description of social systems has brought to communication, which supports new descriptions of belonging. Resulting from the interplay between emergent structural properties of social systems and humans, the latter responded to those structural transformations. Due to new technologies and accelerating movement, new identities of mobile, free and unattached individuals have emerged. The modern world is characterised by changing modes of production and a fundamental reshaping of culture in terms of values, functions, symbols, images, everyday practice and rituals. Having too much information at one's disposal can present an obstacle in terms of exaggerated confusion and dispersion in the individual's self-description. Making deliberate decisions about who we actually are is much more common than before. One can say, there are many more agential capabilities in the hands of individuals than there were in previous decades. Accordingly, identities have become more fluid and reflexively constructed in recognition to the fact that the only factor that enables continuity in the individual's biography and personal narratives is the ability to make cultural choices (Delanty 2000, p. 160).

Considering the new social context signified by global connections and new uncertainties of individualisation, we may increasingly be able to define hybrid identities, adding new dimensions of significance to ourselves. However, this is not an uncontested, linear process. The question remains whether hybridity can only be in the domain of privileged social groups (cf. Bagnoli 2007). It is argued that access to various resources (cognitive and physical) is crucial. The late modern epoch of de-traditionalisation and individualisation put to the foreground the "project of self", that pertains an emphasis on individual self-fulfilment and personal development, "which comes to replace relational, social aims" (Duncan and Smith 2006, p. 2). However, those ideas of individuals' liberation from social structure partly seem to fail to take into account the fact that social forces as social actors are indisputably embedded within structures (Adams 2006; Ritzer 2008; Fligstein and McAdam 2012). There is also a substantial influence of social forces, which may be invisible to individuals. As Brannen and Nilsen (2005, p. 424) argue, "while the lives people live continue to be processually and contextually embedded, people may find the external and structural forces that shape their lives more difficult to comprehend and therefore talk about". What seems to be important is that "social structure is a contingently reproduced set of social conditions, and not a necessary effect of the social totality or something that is historically predetermined"

(Sibeon 2004, p. 57). Therefore, individualised choices and increasing fluidity regarding identifications do not imply the end of structural limitations. Although individuals are not confronted with static social structures typical for pre-modern conditions, they do depend significantly on a structural context. Social environment provides and limits the options among which the individuals are able to choose, and they are far from providing equal options to all individuals.

A variety of resources (i.e. material, social and cultural) conditions the individual's embeddedness in particular social contexts, which also expresses involuntary agential positioning. Social embeddedness determines social imperatives defined by social structure, which in turn provides the reproduction of social systems. Social imperatives are potential causal powers of structural emergent properties, which have a tendency to impinge upon individuals, but can also remain unexercised. They are seen as enablements and constraints, which imply individual agency (Archer 2003). Social imperatives refer to discursive influences, but also to non-discursive ones, to which we do not pay much attention here. As we are interested in the determination of an individual's social embeddedness in the discursive influences acting as a potential trigger on his or her reflexivity, we define discursive influences in the scope of codes.

The inspiration for this approach can be found in Bernstein's restrictive and elaborated codes, but only as the idea that there are different kinds of expression, with consequences for different kinds of meaning. Therefore, codes are a form of "semantic variation" (Hasan 2009). This can be a potential trigger to an individual's cognition but due to the particular aspects of social embeddedness, individuals can be a medium of dissemination (i.e. unconscious dimensions of habitus are crucial in an individual's cognition). It also needs to be said that Archer recognises the role of non-conscious features in the depiction of passive agents, i.e. individuals to whom things happen (Archer 2003). In the individual's reflexivity, an important role is also played by interactional and figurational inter-relations between individuals (cf. Mouzelis 2007). Their constellation is defined by social environment as the 'institutional game' and they are crucial especially in inter-subjective creation of meaning, on which we focus in detail later in the text. The listed social imperatives impinge upon humans and their internal conversation, which can lead to reflexive deliberations.

In order to comprise both the micro and macro levels of social reality and thus take into account causal properties of both emergent entities, we rely on a theory of social fields that we imply on a transnational level. This allows us to consider geographically and culturally dispersed social environments and social forces ensuing from those spaces as well as the individuals who need to possess particular resources to participate in them. All those elements play a particular role in the ability for reflexivity leading to personal identities. Exploring identifications through transnational social fields in a conceptual framework allows a closer examination of the complex interaction between individual practices and transnational, national and local contexts. It enables us to take into account the cultural, social and political horizons that influence the variety of pre-existing dispositions in people's reality, and allows us to investigate how social, economic, cultural and personal backgrounds influence someone's identity negotiations and constructions in the transnational sphere (Gargano 2009, p. 343). It considers the role of the positionality of individuals, individual experiences and reflexive considerations of someone's actions, institutional rules and relevant aspects of international communities and groups. Therefore, it embraces the simultaneity of locality and multiplicity in identifications, while its theoretical implications offer a springboard for empirical research.

3. Transnational social fields

The origins of social field theory have quite a long history. The notion of a field is nowadays widely associated with social phenomena, yet its roots go back to the natural sciences. Martin (2003) argued that Einstein's theory of general relativity technically provided the natural sciences a field theory and inspired the initial considerations of fields in social sciences. In the light of social theories, three main directions progressed in the field theory (ibid.): the social-psychological theory associated most notably with Lewin (1951), the field theory of stratification or domination associated most notably with Bourdieu (1977), and the field theory of inter-organisation relations associated most notably with DiMaggio and Powel (1983).

In recent decades, interest in the concept of social fields has proliferated. According to Fligstein (2001, p. 230), there is an increased interest across various 'new institutional theories' which intend to explain "how social institutions, defined as rules that produce social interaction, come into existence, remain stable, and are transformed". They focus on the construction of local social orders, which could be called 'fields', 'arenas', or 'games', and explores the relationship between actors and the social structures in which they are embedded. However, it has been argued that the new institutionalism has certain limitations regarding conceptualisations, which see fields as interactions between more and less powerful collective groups, while taking into account shared meanings and rules. In order to overcome those limitations, a more social, collective conception of action is needed (Fligstein 2001). Recently, an integrated theory of social fields was offered that explains how stability and change are achieved by social actors in circumscribed social arenas (Fligstein and McAdam 2012). The concept of the social field was widely recognised as having the potential to efficiently confront the issue of agency and structure. It also informed many empirical findings (cf. Fligstein 2001). Through transformations of the social order, globalisation and transnational connectivity, the issue of social fields was also transferred to international and transnational spheres.

It offers explanations for the simultaneity of locality and multiplicity of identities, and can elucidate the situation of many social groups. Transnational social fields seem to enable the consideration of the complex process of perceiving the self and others in this world of movement, and help us to understand contested contemporary identifications. We believe that the concept of social field and particularly the transnational social field can shed light on certain aspects of the relationship between the individual, society and identification, while it challenges methodological nationalism (cf. Levitt and Glick Schiller 2004) while still taking account of the social forces and institutions that greatly influence the individual's "biography" (Giddens 1991). The incorporation of ideas into an analytical approach that consider transnational social fields provides a space to explore identifications that emerge as a result of individual experiences within different national communities or groups, institutional rules and transnational connections.

The concept of the transnational social field emerged from migration studies (Fouron and Glick Schiller 2001; Levitt and Glick Schiller 2004) that focused on how global processes and flows influence transnational processes, highlight issues of agency and community, facilitate the creation of new transnational social networks, and address issues of identity (Moallem 2000; Adler 2000; Tsuda 2002; Riccio 2001; Cohen 2004; Kelly and Lusis 2006; Gargano 2009). The concept's roots can be traced back to the Manchester School of Anthropology where the idea of the field was emphasised in order to explore urbanised localities in conditions of rapid social and political change. Those ideas were elaborated in the seminal work of Nina Glick-Schiller, Linda Basch and Cristina Blanc-Szanton (1994) who defined social fields as a "set of multiple interlocking networks of social relationships through which ideas, practices and resources are unequally exchanged, organised and transformed" (Levitt and Glick Schiller 2004, p. 1009). The notion called into question over-generalised conceptualisations implying a singular set of relations within a field (e.g. Vertovec 2001). The individuals participating in transnational social spaces or fields are in no way a homogeneous group and, accordingly, it was emphasised that there are many ways of "being transnational", in reference to different social spaces (Smith 2002). Individuals move through different social fields (Kearney 1995), that represent a complex set of factors influencing individual practices, attitudes and identifications. The complexity of the internal dynamics of a particular field and the co-influence of a variety of social fields evoked the concept of "power-geometry" (Vertovec 2001) or the new cross-border geography (Sassen 2002) that emphasises the issue of differential embeddedness.

The role of social positioning and power relations was taken into account in the conceptualisation of transnational social fields offered by Levitt and Glick Schiller (2004) who partly built on Bourdieu's idea of the field. In recent decades, a series of Bourdieusian studies concerning international issues have been conducted (e.g. Bühlmann et al. 2013). Although Bourdieu used the concept primarily in a national context (Savage and Silva 2013), he put this query to the fore with his reflections on the transition from the national to the international field (Bühlmann et al. 2013, p. 216). However, certain amendments have to be made in terms of internationalising or transnationalising the idea of the field. Levitt and Glick Schiller (2004), for instance, proposed the concept of social field that differentiates 'ways of being' as opposed to 'ways of belonging'. The former refers to "actual social relations and practices that individuals engage in rather than identities associated with their action". In contrast, "ways of belonging refer to practices that signal or enact an identity which demonstrates a conscious connection to a particular group". Individuals within transnational social fields can combine and incorporate both ways differently in a specific context (ibid., pp. 10–11). Our considerations are inspired by works (e.g. Glick Schiller and Fouron, 2001; Levitt and Glick Schiller 2004) that emphasise that national boundaries do no necessarily overlap or equate boundaries of social fields. Transnational social fields comprise various locations that extend across the borders of two or more nation-states and incorporate their participants in the day-to-day activities of social reproduction (Fouron and Glick Schiller 2001, p. 544). Those conceptualisations of transnational social fields do not differ much from that proposed by Fligstein (2001, p. 108), who sees fields as local social orders or social arenas where "actors gather and frame their actions vis-à-vis one another". As Levitt and Glick-Schiller (2004, p. 10) argue, "in one sense, all (social fields) are local, in that near and distant connections penetrate the daily lives of individuals lived within a locale". However, as they continue, the concept emphasises the division of these connections into local, national, transnational and global ones. Participating within this 'local', an individual may be present in personal networks or receive ideas and information that simultaneously connect them to other networks and information in a nation-state, across the borders of a nation state and globally (ibid., p. 10).

The use of social fields as an analytical framework for the contemporary identification process allows for the incorporation of recent sociologically dominant tropes concerned with identity issues clustered around both self-reflexivity and habitus (cf. Adams 2006). Social fields offer a promising framework for exploring contemporary identifications, which are not merely ascribed and internalised via socialisation processes, but also an instrumental and strategic project. However, it is not just its heuristic potential in considering agency-structure that seems to be of great importance; it also refers to micro-macro phenomena in the social reality and thus affords a more integrative perspective on social processes and social change. The main advantage of the theoretical concept can be seen in how it accords with everyday usage and in its attention to the concrete, even though its definition might be quite tautological (Martin 2003). Social fields offer the examination of concrete social forces in their determination of social imperatives and individuals.

Viewing social fields as arenas or local orders, where "interactions between more and less powerful collective groups according to rules and shared meanings take place" (Fligstein 1997, p. 11), we reach the intermediary level between totality and individuality, where the real substance of social reality can be found (cf. Sztompka 1993, Rončević and Makarovič 2010). Therefore, dynamics within a particular field can be seen as an intermediary level between structures and agents. Social fields are thus a useful concept for exploring identifications in a social world where social, economic and cultural connectivity has increased, and the nature of individual consciousness, people's motivation to pursue their ends, and the extent of their freedom from external influences have become a challenging theoretical and empirical task. It simultaneously enables the consideration of social networks and other social forces and individuals or collective agents as objects of analysis.

Transnational social fields take account of the role of the positionality of individuals, individual experiences and reflexive considerations of people's actions, institutional rules and relevant aspects of international communities and groups. As we explore identifications, the issue is directly connected to individuals and their capability for action. However, as we have already argued, humans are embedded in particular social environments, which entail certain limitations to those capabilities. An additional question is the extent to which individual strategies are in domain of individuals and when they do become collective. We argue that the participation in certain transnational social fields and disposition to particular forms of social, cultural and symbolic resources have certain impact on a habitus that enables individuals to feel more transnational and to form instrumental identities as an adaptation to a changed social context that encourages reflexive deliberations.

First, there are various types and amounts of resources that one needs to possess in order to enter transnational social fields. Individuals participating in transnational social fields are simultaneously embedded in national ones. Their position in the latter influences the possibility of entering the transnational or international spheres. For instance, there are a lot of educated, white-collar, predominantly young and wealthy people who participate in European social fields, which are transnational in nature, (cf. Fligstein 2008). Or, the actors of Swiss international business elites are still part of specific national elite fields that are substantiated and characterized by a concatenation of structural relations between positions that are differently endowed with capital (e.g. Bühlmann 2013, p. 217). It is economic, cultural and social resources that seem to be crucial, while the amount of a particular type of resource can vary. In the case of managerial elites, individuals need to be well educated, to have extended social networks, and to possess significant economic resources in order to participate in the transnational social sphere. In contrast, when it comes to transnational diaspora, the economic resources and education may not be so important, while social networks and cultural capital in the form of narratives of common origin are crucial. On this point, we do not focus on their relation and the role of resources within transnational fields, which influence intra-relations between actors. Social fields are also embedded in a complex web of other fields. The distinction can be made between distant or proximate fields, dependent and interdependent fields or state and non-state fields (McAdam and Fligstein 2012). Participation in transnational social fields is influenced by participation in other (national) social fields that disposes an individual to a lifestyle or a way of living associated with the particular social group from which they originate.

An important issue here, therefore, are different backgrounds of individuals, which reflect the influence of all three mentioned social forces and the role of different types of resources or capital, which is always field-specific and contingent upon the recognition of its value by others (Bourdieu and Wacquant 1992). Individuals incorporate their own histories regarding a particular local and national environment into the transnational sphere, where they interact with each other. They come into contact with a variety of social memories, narratives and values that influence the process of creation of meaning and consequently construction of identity. The latter, however, does not mean that during this process a simple bricolage of identity emerges (e.g. Golob 2014).

While they are a part of transnational social fields, individuals are still (more or less) embedded in national ones. Via socialisation processes they internalise certain cognitive maps, which refer to thick cultural influences, rooted values, and are also a part of their dispositions in a transnational social sphere. They can also be embedded in other social forces concerning national or local spheres, for instance institutional rules or relational topographies of networks (cf. Beckert 2010). In order to explore dynamics of identifications within transnational social fields, one needs to pay attention to the interplay of various social forces, which consist of cognitive frames structuring the perceptions of agents, relational topographies of networks and institutional rules prevalent in the field (ibid.) influencing the subjective self-position and definition within the field. Those forces coincide with social imperatives mentioned above, i.e. discursive influences and figurational relations, but the terminology is used as it allows more concrete examinations of those forces within a particular field. Individuals or social groups who participate in transnational social fields legally belong to particular nation-states and are thus embedded in particular legal and political institutions. It is important to pay attention to how nation-states regulate economic interactions and political processes as they influence social action.

Furthermore, as they participate in a transnational social sphere, their actions are also influenced by particular supranational institutional rules and the topography of transnational social networks. As they interact on the transnational level, they are embedded in various cognitive maps that can offer contested meanings while they communicate through widespread networks. The examination of the role of all three dimensions of an individuals' positioning and acting within a field offers a more comprehensive view on identity construction in the transnational sphere. This element can also comply with different modes of reflexivity as proposed by Archer (2012), who says that reflexivity can be communicative, autonomous, meta and fractured, on which we will elaborate later in Table 1. Therefore, there are also social forces that influence transnational social spheres: institutional rules, which exceed national environments; cognitive maps, which are closer to thin culture, are more subjective and endogenous; and there are also social networks, which are positioned above the national sphere. These discursive influences or codes become increasingly contested. Following Archer (2003), we could say that emergent structural properties offered by the national social sphere become constraints to individuals who orient their purpose towards differing life goals. The transnational sphere, in contrast, offers structural properties, which can be seen as enablements and thus encourage an individual's reflexive deliberations. The agential powers of individuals invoke causal powers of structural properties.

Structural properties on both levels, national and transnational, are a trigger to humans or situated subjects carrying sets of prepositions. Individuals have to negotiate their presence on different levels, which are socially and geographically distant from each other. There is a dissonance between structural forces, a 'clash' between thick and thin cognitive maps, institutional rules, and definitions of relevant resources, which do not merely encourage but rather demand a high level of reflexivity. The combination of transnational and other types of structural dispositions is also a basis of more conscious dimensions of habitus, the influences of which gradually become less significant. Another is the feel of the game, or mediation between individual embeddedness and personal concerns, which leads us to a role of transnational resources.

The term 'Subject' contains a set of prepositions and has different types of resources at its disposal. Due to embeddedness in transnational social structures, there are also forms of transnational resources, which are crucial. Transnational social and cultural resources play an important role in the so-called capability of internal conversation, that influences practical logic. Individuals deliberate upon national and transnational social context according to their capability for internal conversation, which is however heterogeneous and depends on differential access to resources, either cognitive or physical. Reflexivity, which allows a subjective consideration of someone's action, is also a result of embeddedness in the context of differentiated resource. We argue that, in terms of Lash and Urry's (1994) reflexivity winners and losers, participants in transnational social fields are all winners, but to a different extent. They are not a homogenous group, but when compared to individuals embedded only in national social fields, they are winners, as they have at their disposal a great amount of different resources that they can make use of in order to achieve their goals. They have the ability to recognise or to induce the enablements of structural properties and make deliberate decisions or post-reflective choices. Through transnational networks, and using transnational social resources, the individual can distribute economic, symbolic and cultural resources that rely on the resources of two or more countries. These resources yield a more intensive reflexivity and more conscious dimensions of habitus. As we already postulated, the higher the reflexivity is, the more negligible the unconscious dimensions of habitus are.

However, there is another crucial factor, which in the interplay between reflexivity and habitus works in favour to the former: contested figurational relations. As Mouzelis (2007, no pages) argues, in order to understand the relationship between habitus and reflexivity, one needs to consider not only "the dispositional and positional dimensions but also the interactive one of social games". On one side, there is the role/institutional structure of the game and on the other, there are the actual relations between actors. So it is important to take account of the cultural, social and political horizons that influence the variety of pre-existing dispositions in people's reality. They condition and substitute the dispositional elements of habitus. Furthermore, we have to take into account the dialectic relationship between the reflexive, collective and dispositional components of practice. It is important to focus on the existing social networks individuals use to organise their lives (Bottero 2010, p. 20). One needs to consider "the intersubjective nature of practice, and the concrete calls to order that arise from networks of variously disposed agents, whose actions must be accounted for, negotiated and aligned" (ibid., p. 20). Local order (cf. Fligstein 2001) is where individuals take action and simultaneously produce meaning with regard to each other's behaviour emergent through a number of social forces. Let us not forget that fields are also socially constructed phenomena. The important role is played by a shared understanding of: what is going on, who is who in terms of power, what are the rules, and what is the logical sense of the field (e.g. McAdam and Fligstein 2012,

p. 10). The process is determined by an intersubjective consideration through which individuals share their perceptions and beliefs and reframe their accounts of their practice and creation of meaning (Bottero 2010). In the transnational sphere, the figurational relations become contested and require more intensive reflexivity. The figurational relations also define the rules of transnational social games. Therefore, practical logic, which leads to articulation of dispositions, positions, and figurations, leads to intersubjective meaning (cf. Bottero 2010) and results in personal concerns, aspiration and strategies, which lead to transnational instrumental identifications.

Social practice conversely triggers structural forces, and the process continues. Individuals that move within transnational social fields are better equipped to influence social forces. For instance, the influence on institutional rules is clearly evident in the distinction between legal citizens and non-citizens as well as in the case of transnational migrants, who can hold dual citizenship and vote, lobby or finance campaigns in more than one system and can accordingly exert their influence beyond the domain of direct political action (e.g. Glick-Schiller 2005). They can influence their legal and social status as well as their economic and political relations in both locations. Migrants and other transnational actors are able to establish and sustain broad social networks that extend beyond different boundaries and are thus more capable of guiding their actions. Moreover, their cognitive frame allows for greater flexibility and adaptation to the relevant social context. The transnational way of life is not automatically linked to a conscious connection to a certain group and to belonging. But, as Levitt and Glick Schiller (2004) hypothesise, someone with access to a transnational way of belonging is likely to act according to it at some point in their life. Social fields enfold institutions, organisations and experiences that generate categories of identities that in turn are ascribed to or chosen by individuals or groups. A transnational layer of identities can be a consequence but also a deliberate decision. For instance, in the case of transnational migrants, it was shown that individuals can consciously choose and switch between multiple identities (Golob 2009; Repič 2010). It was argued that the success of migrants involved in transnational activities does not depend so much on them renouncing their tradition, culture and language and accepting those of another society (Portes et al. 1999, p. 229). Their success is rather due to them protecting and maintaining their original cultural richness, while also adapting to a additional one when it serves their needs (Portes et al. 1999, p. 229). Identifications could take on an instrumental worth and accordingly play a significant role in an individual's agency in transnational processes. The crossing of a border, whether physical or cognitive, constantly demands a transformation and redefinition of one's identity, while multi-layered and changeable identifications represent an essential and effective strategy for individuals (Repič 2010). According to the increase in global communication, media, consumerism and popular culture, individuals negotiate traditions, memories, and feelings of belonging in a never-ending effort to form and re-form new ambivalent identities. Transnational connections offer important insights into social actions and creation of meaning as they acknowledge individuals' agency whenever the decide how to identify and act, while depending on the context they are engaged in. Transnational social fields are, in a certain manner, spaces of resistance, whereas multi-layered identifications and transnational practices represent a conscious effort to escape the control of capital and state (Guarnizo 1998; Low and Zúñiga 2003) although their influence cannot fully be escaped. As it was argued, transnational individuals or groups are those who "maintain connections, build institutions, conduct transactions and influence local and national events at multiple sites" (Glick Schiller et. al. 1995, p. 48). However, the extent of their success in those terms depends on the possession of various resources and social skills that also influence their negotiation of identities, which conversely offers a source for their formulation of strategies to gain power to control their lives. There is more than one way to be a transnational actor, and the concept of transnational social fields allows a closer examination of different historical backgrounds, social, political and cultural contexts, and social interactions in individuals' creation of sense, which result from the interplay between social forces and intimate revaluations.

The concept of the transnational social field is capable of shedding light on the dynamics of identity construction, which are more specific in the transnational sphere. Entry to a transnational social sphere is not a given for every individual, and being able to add a transnational layer to collective identities can be regarded as the privileged position of a few. A substantial role is played by the individual's ability to access various types of resources: social, economic and cultural. The possession of a selection of resources is essential as it allows to cross over from local and national social fields to transnational ones. The transition between particular fields enables more intensive reflexivity and a consideration of an individual's action as well as of the institutional frames in which they are embedded. Accordingly, transnational individuals have more social skills, which express what people do to attain collective action and give meaning and sense to our lives (cf. Fligstein and McAdam 2012, p. 46). Transnational layers of identities can thus take on instrumental meaning and allow individuals to have greater control over their lives and more easily achieve their goals. Furthermore, the concept of transnational social fields allows an understanding of the transnational context of the different dimensions of social fields relating to cognitive frames, institutional rules and relational topographies of networks (Beckert 2010). It reveals how constant border crossing (physical or imaginary), transnational social interaction and institutions, and an individual's life experiences from the past and other national or local environments shape perceptions of the self and others.

So far, we showed how to investigate identification processes in transnational social fields as such, and illustrated how this configuration leads to more conscious dimensions of habitus, that individuals possess in transnational social fields, whereby reflexivity is more potent and can lead to consciously produced instrumental identifications. The next step is to operationalize the latter. The habitus is not just a theoretical tool, but it is also a tool of investigation. As Wacquant (2011, p. 81) says: "the practical acquisition of those dispositions by the analyst serves as technical vehicle to better penetrate their social production and assembly". It reveals the repertoire of the semantic meanings someone has to his disposal, and the resources to interpret and evaluate them. Instrumental identities are not only the result of deliberate decisions and strategies, but are possible because the strategies chosen can influence structural embeddedness to the extent to which individuals consider it efficient. As we presupposed, when reflexivity is employed often and combined with post-reflexive choices, transnational identifications are more strategic and more supranational in their substance. Identifications are thus increasingly detached from national frames. Because of the noted intertwinement of social forces, which trigger human inner space, unconscious dimensions of habitus become a matter of deliberate negotiations. According to our theoretical framework, the transnational social field is modelled as a coordinate system that maps transnational resources against transnational/non-transnational social forces.

Figure 3.1: Empirical implications of transnational social fields

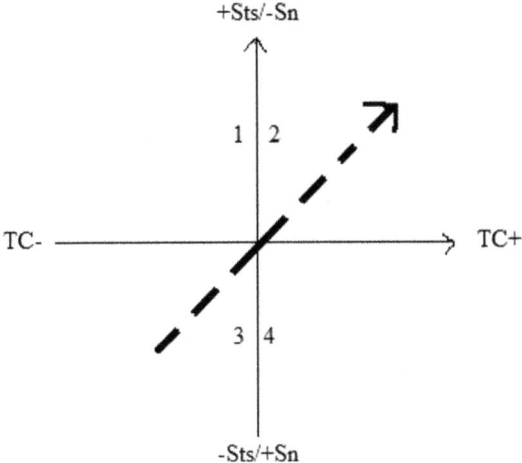

Sts – transnational social forces
Sn – national social forces
TC – transnational resources

The vertical axis represents social forces differentiated against one another. Actors embedded more in transnational social structures in reference to transnational semantic influences are more at the top, while actors wedded more to national social forces in reference to national semantic influences are farther at the bottom. One's position regarding transnational social structuring also reflects the power one possesses in the transnational social field. This coincides with Fligstein and McAdam's (2012, p. 13) idea of strategic action fields, where there can be a tension between "incumbents and challengers". As they propose, incumbents are actors who have most of the power within a field and whose interests tend to be heavily reflected in the dominant organisation of the strategic action field. The purposes and structure of the field are adjusted to their interests. Challengers occupy less privileged positions, but while they recognise the nature of the field and the dominant logic of incumbent actors, they can articulate an alternative vision of the field and their respective position in it. The important role is once again played by socially skilled actors who have the capacity to strategically deploy shared meanings and identities and set the stage for innovative action and even new fields (ibid.). Incumbents are more at the top, while challengers are more at the bottom. The horizontal axis represents transnational resources, including all types of resources taking the transnational form.

The actors who possess more transnational resources (social, cultural, political, economic) are situated more on the right, while actors with less transnational resources are more on the left.

The ability for reflexivity is determined by the horizontal and vertical axis, therefore with the amount of transnational resources and embeddedness in transnational social structures and the detachment of national ones. According to our model, in the second quadrant, the reflexivity is the highest and the unconscious dimension of habitus a regular subject of reconsideration, while in the third one, the reflexivity is the lowest and the habitus works more as schemata for routine actions. The individuals in the second quadrant also deploy the most post-reflexive choices. According to our model, the transnational identifications are the most strategic and instrumental in the second quadrant. The values are specific and relative to the particular field. For instance, even when actors are present in the fourth quadrant, they still have a greater ability for reflexivity and make more post-reflexive choices than actors who are embedded only in national social fields.

To explain why this model works, we intend to focus on a particular transnational social group: EU officials. The framework for further empirical endeavours is as follows: when, for instance, a young trainee starts to work in an office of one of the members of the EU parliament or in the European Commission, s/he is still very much embedded in a national environment, perhaps s/he still studies there, etc. S/he also possesses a relatively low amount of transnational resources. Her/his operators of the feel for the game within a field are heavily influenced by (S_n). Self-description and subsequent actions resulting from operational modes of consciousness follow the equation $(S_{ts}+S_n)*tc$, and work according to national semantic influences, but then proceed through intersubjective meaning, which depends on concrete networks and concrete "'calls to order' that arise from networks of [...] variously disposed agents, whose actions must be accounted for, negotiated and aligned" (Bottero, 2010, p. 20).

Therefore, if we consider field an organised striving (Martin 2003), those trainees tend to become more transnational. They have to articulate their position in both structural dispositions (transnational and national) but gradually orient their strategies and concerns towards being more transnational. Consequently, their identification also becomes more transnational, as being European could be an instrumental decision for them. The European long-term officials, for instance, can be found in the second quadrant. They are mostly embedded in transnational social structures, and possess a great deal of transnational resources. Social structures tied to a national environment lose their influence invoked through habitus. The articulation of their position is linked predominantly to transnational social embeddedness and also their feel of the game within the field is oriented toward more transnational strategies and concerns. In that regard, their ascribed patterns of habitus can be a matter of deliberate consideration. Their practices also have a substantial reverse influence on transnational social structures (they can make post-reflective choices).

4. European social fields

We consider the European Union as a unique phenomenon of supranational governance containing a set of specifics, dilemmas and advantages. The European Union was created as a response to global market competitiveness, a need for political stability and social integration. Its existence reflects the issues of democracy, regional developments and developmental performance of national societies in economic, social and cultural contexts (Adam et al. 2005). The processes of identification reveal the political actions of the Union, the role of various cultural and social politics, as well as different social processes taking place within a supranational entity influenced by both economic and other soft factors, such as social and cultural resources. The issues mentioned play an important role in both the micro and macro levels of the European Union.

In order to present the phenomenon of European (transnational) identifications in the most comprehensive manner, one should not neglect the origins of the concept of European identities, its political roots and cultural implications. In that regard, the notion of Europe comprising a geographical, political and cultural entity seems to be important. In political discourses, the legitimacy of the European Union is often referenced to as 'Europe', while the use of both entities overlaps in common usage. The complex semantic meanings of the word 'Europe' have inevitably led to confused perceptions of the European Union. The emergence of different perspectives initially began with the consideration of Europe as a political entity in the sixteenth century in the context of the Muslim threat to Christianity. The idea of Europe was broadly associated with the notions, values and ideals of civilisation, relying on and drawing from the fact that it is European (Delanty and Rumford 2005).

The existence of European identity as a concept inspired a myriad of academic, professional and political contributions to the matter. It is a complex and ambiguous issue denoting multiple levels of perceptions of European space as geographic and imagined territory on one hand, and the European Union as a political and social entity on the other. Accordingly, it can be tackled from different angles, which includes the exploration of various historical, economic, political and social contexts that influenced its construction. The European Union is not identical to Europe, although both terms are being used as synonyms by many people every day. Europe is certainly a much broader concept than the European Union, as feeling European does not necessarily result in a support for the latter (cf. Buecker

2006). As Burgess (2002, p. 468) postulates, if boundaries of both entities overlap, it would be a situation in which

> [...] every conceivable property of Europe, every individual, every collectivity, every political, economic, social, cultural entity were included in toto in the European Union, the entire population of the continent, and the continent itself, its soil, water and air, every beast, from the last brown cow of Flanders, to every wild boar of Tuscany, were a part of the institutional apparatus of the EU.

The issue of identification with an ambiguous and not clearly defined entity inevitably leads to many interpretations, prepositions and assumptions. The European Union is not a Europe but it can hardly be reduced to only a set of regulations. One should not neglect that in principle, the motivation for European integration is based on the idea of the united Europeans. The political legitimacy of the EU thus draws on discourses wherein the political unity of Europe is inextricably intertwined with the European continent. The political mobilisation of the concept has increased the importance of its meaning. The Europe that refers to the EU can be perceived as an "imagined community" in the making (Sassatelli 2002, p. 436). Therefore, the European Union built its foundation on the images of Europe and while it understands those images, it also intends to conceptualise the Union, or at least its significant part.

The concept of Europe is therefore a complex plethora of meanings. Considering historical narratives, it is noticeable that the notion is built on specific cultural frames referring to the common religious framework based on the Judaeo-Christian tradition. Further, the raison d'etre of the idea of Europe is the tradition of Enlightenment rationalism (e.g. Tomšič 2012). Europe as a concept ensued from the recognition of certain European values, which played an important role in the initial endeavours of the European Union's architects. As Schuman (2003, p. 11) emphasised, the idea of Europe, which can unite all European nations and provide a common path of prosperity, security and peace, is the idea that illustrates the foundations of European civilisations. In that regard, it is inextricably tied to democracy and Christian doctrine, which should provide successful European integration. Common European values and culture formed the spiritual basis from which the modern western society emerged, with parliamentary democracy and market economy presenting two major institutional components (Tomšič 2012, p. 630). The assemblage of values that embrace the notions of freedom, tolerance, respect for human personality and the ability to advocate personal rights, constitute the essence of European fundamental values. They are an essential component that induced the emergence of democracy and its consolidation on an European scale (ibid.). On that basis we can speak about European patriotism, which advocates an united Europe, its values and cultural heritage.

The idea of the common European ground, however, collides with certain ambiguities. For instance, narratives of the common values, prospects and developmental ideals refer to the construction of the European West and emphasise the distinction between European West and East. Accordingly, the question appears to be what and where Europe actually is. The ambiguity of the concept undermines the legitimacy of the European Union, which it draws from the idea of Europe. If both entities were equal, the issue of European identity might be less contested and ambiguous. However, it is the concept of Europe itself that contains many non-geographical meanings involving various political, cultural, and economic aspects (Ifversen 2002). As Delanty (2000, p. 132) asserts, Europe is a geographical entity that is "simply too large and too abstract to be imagined in any meaningful sense". The Encyclopaedia Britannica defines Europe as the "second smallest of the world's continents, composed of the westward-projecting peninsulas of Eurasia and occupying nearly one-fifteenth of the world's total land area" (Ifversen 2000, p. 2). The definition, which at first sight might seem as a straightforward geographical description, is constructed on a conceptual and ideological basis that ensues from a certain image of the world. The continent has come to play an important role in what Lewis and Wigen (1997) term "metageographical mythology" (Ifversen 2000, p. 2). Europe is commonly accepted as one of the seven continents, although it is actually a part of the larger Eurasia. Specific geographical features, high mountains and broad rivers, present a sort of natural border between both parts especially in the east, but in a political sense the division between the two is still not entirely clear. The ambiguity of the borders are evident in the present negotiations for membership of the European Union, with Turkey remaining the most contested country to be accepted. The cultural boundaries between continents have changed according to certain political interests. Certain countries, which were many centuries a part of Asia, North America or Africa, are now members of the European Union. For instance, Cyprus, which is lies close to Minor Asia, Malta, which was perceived as an island of North Africa for centuries, or Iceland, placed near to Greenland, draw their political legitimacy of being a member state of the EU not only from political but also from cultural basis. The economic and political interests are widely intertwined with the cultural and historical discourses which influenced the political borders and imaginary boundaries of Europe. Conceptual boundaries meet natural borders to a mostly on the Caucasus Mountains and the Ural, which divide the continent of Eurasia into a western and eastern part. Uncontested demarcation of both parts of the continent can also be found in the Caspian and Black Sea and on the water routes connecting the Black and Aegean Sea. The northern, western and, in part, southern borders are seemingly more clearly defined, but viewing the imperial history of some European countries, one can see that Europe once extended to many parts of the world. Furthermore, it's notable that the borders of Europe are not only blurred because of the socio-cultural factors defining the external borders, but also in the light context of internal historical divisions (cf. Makarovič 2008). Therefore, there's an importance to the boundaries dividing Europe itself. The first historically notable division was the northern part of the Roman limes, which however did not dramatically influence the subsequent political and socio-cultural development of the area. The crucial division was made by the Theodosius line that divided the Roman Empire into western and eastern parts. A disruption of the empire still coincides with the present-day division between the western forms of Christianity and eastern Orthodoxy. Another important division can be attributed to the Ottoman line, which signified the boundary between Christianity and Islam. Representing a boundary between Occident and Orient, it still plays an important role in collective images of Europe (Said 1996). In the following era, other divisions between West and East also took place, which have not yet completely disappeared in common discourses of Europe, and still have a distinct impact on the development of the countries in question (Adam et al. 2005). This dates back to early industrialisation in the nineteenth century and the subsequent political division, hallmarked by the Iron Curtain (more on internal European borders in Davies 1996). Considering the ambiguous external borders and the existence of multiple 'Europes' within these borders, the common identity is certainly a contested notion. As Stråth (2002, p. 388) points out, "the meanings of Europe are a discourse of power on how to define and classify Europe, on the frontiers of Europe, and on similarities and differences". For our discussion, it is important to stress that European identity always reflected prevailing discourses and perspectives of political and intellectual elites on Europe, and was thus conceptualised on a different basis in different historical periods.

The term 'Europe' reaches far back in a history, but, as it has been argued, the idea of Europe as a political and cultural entity is quite a recent phenomenon (Boer 1995, p. 52). The origin of the term itself dates back to antiquity. The word 'Europe' primarily referred to a mythological character, a Phoenician beauty abducted by the god Zeus who took the appearance of a white bull (Mastnak 1996, p. 12). Nowadays, it has come to be an important symbol of European history, legacy and heritage. The European Union used a mythological narrative as a symbol of European integration. Noticeably, the web portal of the European Union is named after her.

Further, several memorial coins, such as the Belgian European Expansion coin worth ten Euro has been furnished with her image, and her name is also printed on postage stamps referring to the 'United Union'. However, it remains questionable whether the continent was actually named 'Europe' by the Greeks (Mastnak 1998, p. 47). In general, 'Europe' was used to define ancient Greece and its parts, and it was not until the fifth century, when Herodotus used the term 'Europe' in defining more than just geographical territory. But his definition did not exceed the scope of a geographical description (Fischer 1957, cf. Mastnak 1998). It was not before the times of Charlemagne that the notion gained its political dimension, although it was still not widely used until the end of the fourteenth century (Fischer 1957, in Mastnak 1998). In that period, the term 'Europe' gained a more intensly emotional meaning. Increasingly, it started to be used as a substitute for the Christian community: 'Christianitas'. In the era of Charlemagne, for the first time, the meaning of the word 'Europe' encompassed not only the Latin west of the continent, but also Eastern European countries (Mastnak 1998). The meaning of the term has reached not just political but also cultural semantic fields. During their conflict with the Turks, so-called Europeans defended not only a religion but also a particular lifestyle.

The Enlightenment and the Industrial Revolution brought a decisive acceleration to the change in perspective of Europe, which provided the conglomeration of new ideas. Europe and Christendom were no longer an equal expression, and 'Europea' became associated with the notion of civilisation. Although the term 'Europe' did not describe the continent as whole and excluded the Eastern parts (Stråth 2002), the conception of civilisation generally had a positive connotation. It coincided with the increasing sense of European superiority, which was on the rise along with imperialist tension. In the time of imperial conquests, the important 'Others', serving as an element of identification, also extended to colonised populations living in other continents. European travellers, explorers, and scientists brought from their travels various picturesque descriptions about people living in colonies and other parts of the world, which helped to sustain the image of superiority of Europeans. Convinced of the primacy of European civilisation, they collected so-called scientific evidence to confirm those images, and were thus actively involved in creating European boundaries (more in History of Europe 1995). However, due to internal political conflicts, the only thing that European nations really had in common was a belief in European supremacy over the rest of the world. As Boer et al. (1995, p. 55) argue, this was a paradoxical situation, as the era of rising nationalism was also the time of confidence and belief in European supremacy. This was a period of endless European self-pride and epoch-making European expansion. Progress in various areas of political, economic and cultural areas came to be regarded as a synonym for European civilization, and it was not until the Great War of 1914 that this simplistic association ceased to be a dominant idea. After that turning point in European history, a sense of destruction permeated Europe, and as Boer et al. (1995) say, 'Europe' was associated predominantly with degeneration and decline. In the short period of 1914 and 1945, two world wars claimed tens of millions of dead and wounded. It was a time of immense political and social upheavals and radical transformations in all areas of life. As Bugge says (1995), it was an era of extremes, which broke the European sense of global superiority and brought them close to fatigue. In particular, World War II dramatically changed the position of Europe on the global map. The heritage of totalitarian regimes and the foreign intervention undermined conceptions of European civilisation. A decisive contribution to the loss of the dominance and supremacy of Europe was also made by the Holocaust, which remains a trauma in Europe's collective memories.

In the ruins of World War II, those constructions of superiority lost their relevance. The heritage of totalitarian regimes and the intervention of the United States undermined the conceptions of European civilisation. Political and social instability generated new conceptual groundings. A need for economic cooperation among European countries encouraged new political initiatives in European integration, which lead to the current European Union. Since the very beginning of European integration, the support and the loyalty of the people turned out to be a vital component of economic and political cooperation. The project of increasing the success of integration has thus become tightly interwoven with the role of common European history, heritage and culture. As Jacques Delor once said "nobody falls in love with a common market, you need something else". The idea of common European identity offered a sufficient tool for political elites in their efforts to legitimise the existence of the European Union in the eyes of its citizens (Shore 2004). An escalating interest in European identity coincided with the concerns of the architects of the European Union, who failed to build the foundations for a cohesive European demos. After World War II, Europe was forced to come to terms with the dark side of its colonialism and nationalism, which had led to that military conflict. As the era of imperial rule was over, Europe lost its leading position in the world (cf. Stråth 2002). After the war, the new global forces, such as the USA and the Soviet Union, extensively intervened in European integration and in imaginary constructions of European identity. Both countries took the patronage over particular parts of Europe. Through the implementation of the Marshall Plan of post-war reconstruction, the U.S. acquired significant political influence in Western Europe, while the Soviet Union extended the communist bloc in Central and Eastern Europe. As Stråth (2002, p. 388) says, "the intensified European integration went hand in hand with a growing political search for the roots of common Europeanness". The beginnings of the unification of European countries were primarily based on economic cooperation, treating integration as a subsequent side effect. In the foreground stood the mostly mechanical capitalistic idea that a successful space of freedom and security in Europe would emerge directly from a liberalised economy (Mokre 2007). However, the increased diversity within the Union has become a strong challenge. In order to increase its legitimacy and credibility and to improve its image in the eyes of Europeans, the European Union and its predecessors invested vast amounts of money and energy into various projects to establish a European identity among citizens. In that regard, European identity played a specific role in terms of boosting the reputation and creating a positive image of the EU. This particular conception of European identity is supposed to induce an emotional response, associated with the political advance of EU institutions and authorities. A stronger European identity should thus encourage Europeans to become more active citizens, defending the EU and fostering its future. Consequently, the European identity has become an important element in the political discourses of the EU (cf. Shore 2004).

In order to transmit and consolidate specific images about Europe and the European Union among its citizens, the official political discourses communicate through various cultural policies, media and political projects. The central idea was to link the political entity to Europe as a whole. The concept of Europe provided legitimacy to the European Union, while from the very beginning of European integration the support and the loyalty of the people turned out to be an important component of economic and political cooperation. The first political efforts to build a common European community based on cultural and social imaginaries was the Marshall Plan launched in 1947. Its objectives were primarily oriented towards organising and financing the reconstruction of a continent that lay in ruins after World War II, but a kind of common consciousness, substantiated by common material goals and the horrors of war, also emerged. As Burgess (2002) postulates, the primary economic principles of integration were partly based onthe existence of a certain European collectivity and identity, as the tragedies and catastrophes Europe had endured were not only economic, but cultural and social as well. This is evident in the words of Robert Schuman, who proposed normative ideas of a common European identity based on European culture. In his memoirs "For Europe", he referred to Europeans having made the 'choice' of Europe as the fruit of a collaboration of 'spirits' (Schuman, 1964, p. 23, cited in Burgess 2002, p. 465). Schuman, Monnet and the other original architects of the European Union also saw the institutional form as a wayto re-establish a common European mindset and thus to contribute to European harmony. In order to justify the constitution of the European Coal and Steel community, Schuman drew from the universalistic principles recorded in the Declaration of the Rights of Man and Citizen and connected that document with the 1951 Treaty of Paris (Schuman 1964, p. 27, Burgess 2002, p. 476). The Treaty of the European Coal and Steel Community sought to unite the fragmented peoples of Europe under the umbrella term of 'the European', a "cultural value-complex that recognizes implicit European unity in a divided continent, possessing the power to unite the most elementary form of cooperation, around the cold materiality of coal and steel" (Burgess 2002, pp. 476–477).

In the following years, an increasing interest in European identity coincided with the concerns of the architects of the European Union, but still failed to create the foundations for a cohesive European demos. In times of tangible crisis and tensing of internal and external relations, the issue of European identity gained increased importance. It is not coincidental that European identity was first designed and decided upon at the Copenhagen EC summit in December 1973 (European Commission, 1973). As Strath (2002) says, the purpose of the meeting was connected to the unexpected crisis. Consequently, the concept of 'European identity' gained its importance through concerns linked to the price of dollar and oil and presented an instrument for stabilising and consolidating the position of Europe in the global order. In that manner, the 'European identity' was traced out in an attempt to establish a tripartite European order of corporatist bargaining, which would replace the devastated national economies embracing the unity of Nine (ibid.). In the year 1973, the Declaration of European Identity was established, which defines various dimensions of the European identity regarding common heritage, interests and special obligations within the community. It also embraces the idea of European unification, internal unity and coherence in delimitation to the rest of the world (Declaration on European Identity, also e.g. Burgess 2002, p. 478). The European identity also recognised the rule of law, representative democracy, social justice and respect for human rights as its fundamental elements (Copenhagen Summit Declaration 1973). In the following year, the Paris Summit Conference endorsed the idea of European identity. The Conference also concretised the idea by defining specific policy objectives (Kostakopoulou 2001, p. 44). Consequently, the basis for cultural policy was created, followed by many political initiatives and programmes with the specific aim to support European cultural integration by promoting an European identity for citizens and for the rest of the world.

Consequently, the European identity and cooperation among European citizens can be primarily seen a project of the elites, not directly related to the people, their own imaginaries and identity constructions. Although many efforts were made to establish a common European identity, it can hardly be said that a collective European identity exists. However, as Checkel and Katzenstein argue (2009), it is important to distinguish between European identity in the form of political projects and of social processes. What seem to be important are certain social processes on the transnational level that could have an impact on the identifications with the European Union. In this book, we focus on the European Union as the supranational unit representing the most suitable approximation of wider European space. While we do not attempt to equate both phenomena, the European Union is nevertheless far from being merely an economic and political entity. It has been argued that the EU does not only increasingly define what is meant by 'European', but also to whom or to what this term can be attached. It also attempts to fill 'Europeanness' with specific post-national liberal and substantive values (Risse and Maier 2003, p. 71, Risse 2004, p. 256). Although the European Union is often reasonably seen as a project of political elites serving to fulfil certain economic and political goals, and as a bureaucratic apparatus existing far removed from people's everyday lives, it also enables new ways of cooperation among people, which could lead to a new means of identification. It remains indisputable that the European Union is a group of sovereign national states, which bring their own economic and political interests and cultural meanings into integrated political union. However, one should also take into account that almost eighty per cent of the legislation is unified, and that especially when contrasted to countries of other continents, the EU is recognised as a specific political formation. The European Union made possible a formation of not just the economic and political space, but also of a social space. This requires the exploration of structural questions of social classes, income, gender and racial inequalities, social networks and ways of mobility, as well as a consideration of existing perspectives on public opinion, political participation and mobilisation by the sociology of the European Union (Favell and Guiraudon 2009, p. 555). At first sight, the studies on identifications seem to be excluded from the proposed framework, as they are derived predominantly from the constructivist turn within European Union studies. However, our challenge is linked exactly to the aforementioned dilemma. We would like to approach identifications within a framework of structural forces and social integration, which, in the light of increased social complexity, put forward new questions about complementarity, operations between members of society and the structure of the system.

Foremost, we would like to avoid essentialist approaches, addressing the European identity on the basis of national understanding of political, economic, social and cultural formations of people. While emphasising the role of common European history, heritage and culture as the key elements of European identity, it is closely linked to political interests that strive for a more successful integration of the European Union. Similarly, caution should be exercised towards more recent ideas of the European Commission that consider the European Union a plurality of cultures (Mokre 2007). We do not reject their conceptions, because they give a pivotal role to the existence of multiple identities as a result of the world of flux where differences are cultural features. Still, they insufficiently explain layers of European identity amongst others. The essentialist ideas of the European Union as an imagined community based on national conceptual roots or more recent ideas seeing Europe as a diversity of cultures say more about the work of particular institutions, integration projects or cultural politics on national or supranational levels, than about European identity itself (Sasatelli 2002; Mokre 2007). Therefore, our interest is primarily focused on social processes, while political projects are seen in a broader context, as a substantial component of the contemporary world that influences a variety of social realities.

This text is based on the presumption that particular social processes at the transnational level enable identifications with the European Union and common European space. In order to comprehend the complexity of social conditions that influence contemporary, especially European, identification, one needs to pay attention to two things. First, those identifications take place in a changed transnational environment, which allows specific types of social spaces to emerge, where identities can be constructed and imagined. Those social spaces are subjected to the influence of many forms of individualisation and globalisation, which challenges traditional, collective identities. Transnational social practices and the participation of individuals in European transnational networks and institutions play an important role in the development of these identifications. It is important to recognise and evaluate several factors and social processes that potentially influence attachment to European space. Second, participation in transnational social spaces, which is a basis for European transnational identities, is not a given fact for all inhabitants or citizens of the European Union; therefore, not everyone can participate in such spaces.

The important presumption of the text is this: Participation in transnational social spaces, which is seen as a basis for European transnational identities, is not a common feature of all citizens of the European Union. This unavoidably leads to the concept of transnational social fields. In an important analysis of the relationship between transnational interactions and European identity, Fligstein (2008) stressed the importance of social fields regarding politics, business, education, and civic associational life in order to make Europeans. Considering this, we employ the concept of European (transnational) social fields to deepen the understanding of the complex and ambiguous issue of European identifications. Although there are many studies that emphasise the role of transnational connections in European integration and identification, this study attempts, by employing the issue of transnational social fields, to clarify whether and under what conditions transnational interactions actually contribute to a subjective manifestation of Europeanisation (cf. Mau and Büttner 2009) and influence individual identifications (also e.g. Golob and Makarovič 2012).

Transnationality in this context does not imply a denial of nationality but rather its upgrading. The examined identifications, on the one hand, express the influence of national frames and more deeply rooted semantic meanings, while on the other handthey imply contested supranational, rootless belongings. In the case of the European Union, the influence of national social environments is reflected in a variety of different perceptions of the European Union as well as in different options to enter the transnational European sphere and to construct instrumental identifications. Accordingly, it is crucial to shed a light on contexts that express historical, political and cultural semantic fields, influence European imaginaries, and thus offer the wider understanding of European identifications.

We assume that individual perceptions of supranational communities and transnational identifications are conditioned by geographical, cultural and political contexts, which are inherited through particular national horizons. Accordingly, the comparison of the member states of the European Union is, for instance, considered a highly illuminating component for the exploration of identifications, since it reveals a variety of cultural, social and political factors. While we argue that no homogeneous European identity exists, we encourage the formation of new perspectives on identifications in contemporary social realities, which are closely related to the changes and transformations on the global and local level.

In order to substantiate the theoretical assumptions, the empirical part of this study attempts to show that the contemporary identification processes that occur in transnational social spheres can be instrumental and strategic. The role of habitus is present on the unconscious level and during routine action, but in certain social conditions, it is negligible. Social imperatives trigger an individual's deliberate modes of consciousness. Reflexivity can relate to or increase a particular mode of reflexivity using Archer's formulation to recognise communicative, autonomous or meta-reflexive modes. Particularly, while the last two modes are exercised, the identifications as an intention enable morphogenesis, which is progressive and reflects the actors' ability to influence the social setting according to their internal conversation. For individuals who stay within national frames, the influence of primarily ascribed habitus over identifications is more common; they are predominantly a medium of dissemination of unconscious mental operations of the inner psychical space. They remain in their involuntary agential position and mediate social and cultural emergent properties without changing their positions inside their social or cultural structures. They exact primary agency or their mode of reflexivity can be communicative. Their identifications, even if they are a product of reflexive deliberation, contribute to morphostasis. In the contemporary era of late modernity, the latter situation should be rare. We presuppose that individuals who participate in transnational social spheres are much more actively influencing social setting than those wedded solely to national frames. However, there are also differences amongst the first group.

Table 1.1: *The basic schema for the role of social spheres in identifications*

	Modes of reflexivity	The role of habitus	The possibility of systemic change
National semantic influences	Humans are predominantly medium of semantic dissemination or rarely take stance – communicative reflexivity	primarily ascribed dispositions are highly – medium important	Morphostasis (social structures remain unchanged)
Transnational semantic influences	The dominant mode of reflexivity is 'communicative reflexivity', but also 'autonomous and metareflexivity'	primarily ascribed is medium – low important	Morphogenesis (actors are reproducing, changing the initial social structures)

The social spheres, be they national and transnational, are perceived as social environments in a broader sense, not limited to physical spaces or communities. For instance, one who is participating in a national social sphere is not necessarily living within borders of that particular nation. A collectively socially constructed or imagined community, beyond Anderson's (1983) conceptualisation of national states, comes into existence through a specific form of communication tied to collective or cultural memory. This process is regarded as a result of structural coupling between humans and social systems. The semantics provided by both emergent entities result in a cultural memory that provides a tool of self-description for both, social systems and humans. However, using the term 'collective memory' can lead us to slippery ground, as there is a range of definitions determining its meaning. Accordingly, Assman (2008, p. 55) disaggregates the abstract notion of collective memory to distinguish among different formats wherein memory processes operate, "such as family memory, interactive group memory, and social, political, national, cultural memory" (cited in Raj Isar, Viejo-Rose, Anheier 2011, p. 8). Family or interactive memory is grounded on lived experiences, while political and cultural memory must be "grounded on the more durable carriers of external symbols and representations" (ibid.). Various institutions, such as libraries, museums and archives provide this by storing cultural contents and images. Cultural memory is distant from everyday life and preserves the store of knowledge of unity and peculiarity of a group (Assman 1995, p. 129). The substance of cultural memory is defined through communication of social systems which condition enablements and constraints of social forces, while, as a result of structural coupling, also express mode and intensity of reflexivity, thus reversing the process. Cultural memory should be seen as a particular form of mediated action of human agents who make use of cultural repertoires or cultural tools (cf. Wertsch and Bilingsley 2011).

The availability of cultural tool kits depends on agents' positions in social structures specific to a certain time and place (Wertsch 1998, Wertsch and Bilingsley 2011, p. 29). Humans make use of the cultural repertoires stored in structural semantics. Cultural manifestations are sustained and communicated by texts, rituals, names of places, heritage and language. The most important, fundamental and influential sets of 'mnemonic tools' are narratives, which provide means of distributing knowledge and memory (Wertsch and Bilingsley 2011, p. 31). Nowadays, cultural layers of semantics can be interpreted as an interplay between "thick and thin" cultural substances, that also influence a process of transmission of cultural memory. The notion of thick and thin culture refers to a conceptualisation by Mischler and Pollack (2003), who define culture as a continuum with two idealized endpoints; more basic orientations, for instance identities or orientation toward more fundamental social objects, such as nation, religion, and ethnicity, are according to their model located closer to the conceptual core, where culture is thicker. Less fundamental orientations, such as attitudes, would be located further away from the core, where culture is thinner (Mischler and Pollack 2003, pp. 8–9). Thin cultural layers of semantics refer to narratives and images, which are not only reframed and reproduced. They are contested and thus put into question through new images, which play a central role in the creation of individual and collective identities. A construction of new memories that better suit contemporary cultural complexities seems to be crucial (e.g. Raj Isar, Viejo-Rose, Anheier 2011, p. 9).

An network of cultural influences placed on a continuum of thick and thin cultural endpoints is linked to transformed processes of memory transmission. As Nora (2011, p. ix) highlights, in order to understand fundamental changes in contemporary society, one can incorporate a distinction between transmitted memory and acquired memory as postulated by Walter Benjamin. The former entails information of our existence in the world, our ways of thinking and of conducting our lives. Further it entails how this information is handed down from one generation to the next, and it includes what is perceived as history. It is linked to thick cultural sediments and operates as a sort of imperative. It does not encourage human reflexivity. In contrast, acquired memory is what happens to an individual alone, and it has become increasingly significant in human life. It thus implies changed semantics, which are more substantiated with thin cultural sentiments.

The issue of cultural memory again brings us to the more important role of imagination in social life, and as Appadurai (1996, p. 31) suggests, to grasp this new role, we need to bring together the idea of the imagined community (e.g. Anderson 1983) and the idea of the imaginary as a constructed landscape of collective aspirations. Both are increasingly involved in mobility and interconnected with transnational social and cultural processes. He offered the perspectives of global scapes, which are not "objectively given relations that look the same from the very angle of vision", but imagined worlds of historically situated imaginations of people and groups around the world. Their embeddedness in different political, cultural, economic and social contexts conditions how they encounter flows, from which they construct the world view (ibid., p. 33). The differentiations between national and transnational spheres are tied to the context and the flows that influence the imagination of someone's social environment. Although the world is inevitably interconnected in all aspects of social life, they are not necessarily equally present in imagined worlds. Each type of a sphere (national or transnational) expresses a predominant variety of social forces tied to discursive codes and figurational relations or, as Beckert (2010) says, institutional rules, network topographies and cognitive frames. A national social sphere signifies structural properties predominantly limited to a national level, while a transnational or supranational sphere reaches beyond national boundaries. All three social forces are a part of the interplay between potential structural properties and reflexive deliberations. Here we explore identifications in the transnational sphere composed of specific European social spaces or fields where particular social forces and agential dynamics can be observed. The European Union is far from being a mere political construction but it is also a social space that is "structurally sustained and socially reproduces in order to survive" (Favell and Guiraudon 2009, p. 569). The simultaneous influence of national and supranational or transnational structural layers evokes the question of whether the combination of social forces pertains to the common social structure of the EU. It has been argued (Mau and Mewes 2012) that a European social structure exists, which is an emergent, macro-societal formation. The core elements of its formations, which are a basis of internal homogeneity, of shared social space and the density of social ties among national European societies, are: a) structured diversity, b) processes of convergence and divergence, and c) horizontal links between national societies (ibid., p. 352). The emergent European structure is diverse and composed of different layers, but that does not mean that all citizens or inhabitants of the European Union are embedded in all layers, which is significant for the ability and willingness to identify with the EU.

Recently, there have been many debates on transnational connections, individual participation and their positive impact on European integration and identity formation. The horizontal Europeanization and transnational exchange are considered a driving force in the creation of new identifications. However, those debates also revealed many weaknesses of such connections. It became obvious that transnational connections are highly stratified across society (Fligstein 2008; Mau and Büttner 2009), and European integration has become severely challenged by increased economic uncertainty and competition, and massive immigration flows (Kuhn 2011). It has become obvious that increasing transnational social interaction has made the EU a shared location of interests and one of many social, cultural, and economic exchanges; however, the extent to which those exchanges are visible and available to the general European public is highly questionable. Social stratification plays an important role in that regard. As Fligstein (2008, p. 2) expressively says: "What has struck me most about the creation of a European society is the degree to which people in Europe are unaware of it".

The majority of European citizens almost completely remain within the boundaries of their nation-state (Fligstein 2008; Mau and Büttner 2009). We argue that the more an individual is embedded in transnational social forces and removed from national ones, the more he or she is able (and willing) to identify with the EU. The variety of layers of social forces creates a genuinely European social space, but the majority of European citizens remain excluded. Therefore, certain conditions need to be fulfilled in order to enter the European transnational social space. Diez Medrano has, for instance, gone so far as to call for the emergence of transnational European groups, "i.e. groups of European citizens across borders whose behaviour and consciousness denote solidarities that transcend their (sub)national affiliations as representatives of European society" (Diez Medrano 2008, cited in Favell and Guiraudon 2009, p. 561).

Taking into account the role of participation in a transnational social sphere in identification with the EU, one can see it is not just social stratification or access to different resources that influences the intensity of identifications with the EU. Semantics that substantiate the individuals' perceptions in terms of structural coupling and consequently influence someone's concerns and identifications play an important part. In our case, semantics reflect the intertwining of local, national and transnational cultural frames that influence the interpretation of someone's position in his/her social environment and orient his/her actions. An individual's European identification can also be significantly influenced not only by their personal experiences and social stratifications but also, for instance, by the abundance of media, political, economic, expert and other discourses that influence people beyond their direct personal experience. In these processes, national elites may play a significant role, as demonstrated, for instance, by Adam et al. (2009).

Our claim is that construction of identities with the European Union is heavily influenced by thin cultural sentiments, and the transmission of new images and narratives that contest traditional forms of collective identities. Acquired memory plays the important part. Those identifications are a result of contemporary processes influenced by the growth of global communication, mobility, media, consumerism and popular culture (cf. Favell 2005; Fligstein 2008), which take part in a global or transnational sphere, and allow fluid and multi-layered identifications to be realized.

4.1. Towards the insights from the field

The following chapter attempts to examine identifications with the European space from a bottom-up perspective. It focuses on individuals and their experiences and narratives. First, we would like to show who the people who can identify with the European Union actually are, what the role of transnational practices is in those processes, and how important the simultaneous influence of social forces is. Furthermore, we intend to shed light on transnational identifications by illustrating concrete practices of individuals. As we argued throughout the study, the presence in the European transnational sphere seems to be crucial to add an

European layer to the 'marble cake' of identity. Therefore, what individuals are able to move freely? Why are they migrating through European countries, and is this a successful strategy? How do they cope with cultural differences, and how do they influence perceptions of a common European space and identification? Does their desire and eagerness to travel and to move always translate into a readiness or even an enthusiasm to identify with the European Union?

There are earlier studies that can help us to ellaborate on some answers. One is an interesting research done by the PIONEUR group, an international network of social scientists and research centres funded by the European Commission (Fifth Framework Programme). Their findings showed that, first of all, European citizens seem to be exceptionally unwilling to move and live abroad, despite whatever opportunities they have. However, there is a increasing tendency towards cross-border mobility and travel of all kinds, which pertains especially to a highly motivated, determined and ambitious generation of new Europeans. The data, which was obtained through the aforementioned research focusing on the five largest European member states (France, Germany, Great Britain, Italy and Spain), reveal that EU movers are a quite 'unique but not unitary population', composed of diverse backgrounds such as retirees and traditional working class migrants (PIONEUR group, undated, p. 10).

The majority of intra-European migrants are young, highly educated, show a high level of cognitive mobilisation and originate from an upper-middle class background. The main reasons for migration aren't economic interests but rather intimate motives, cross-national marriages or personal relationships. What seems to be important is that 'EU movers' contribute to strengthening and reinforcing the legitimacy of the EU and its overall positive image. "They form a 'carrier group' of European identity, the living testimonials of an ever closer Union" (PIONEUR group, undated, p. 10). Those individuals seem to integrate well into their new country of residence, but their mobility does not as such contribute to the striking upgrade in status, nor to the opposing process of downwarding social trajectories. Furthermore, the study shows that "political dividends of geographical mobility within the EU are clearer than the economic benefits [...] EU movers are specialists in border-crossing, not in class-crossing" (ibid., p. 11).

Another important attempt to illustrate the human dimension of European integration is an ethnographic study conducted by Favell (2008), who attempts to describe and to analyse a small but symbolically significant population that is establishing and building the new European society. The group is called 'Eurostars', denoting free movers able to take advantage of the opportunities offered by the legislation of the European Union. They are well educated, and want to be successful in their lives. They are individuals who wish to transcend the national social environment. As Favell (2008, p. 10) says, their mobility is sometimes "all about regional movement over small distances separated by large national boundaries". They build lives according to careers, social networks, personal relationship and families that reach beyond the constraints of their nation-states. They live in large European cities called 'Eurocities', which allow and offer that kind of living. Cities such as London, Brussels and Amsterdam present a specific kind of society that is not rooted in national traditions or in a singular thick culture but has a particular cosmopolitan, open-minded nature. A common background of Eurostars is their predominantly provincial origin that drives them to move in order to escape from national constraints. As Favell (2008, p. 116) says,

> "The Eurostars could in fact be true cosmopolitans: pioneering a realistic, attainable, and materialised kind of denationalised life, in the rare space opened up by the Europeanizing dimensions of global cities."

The European social space presents an alternative path to new ways of living in certain circumstances. It is indisputable that, due to changes in European policies, people interact socially in a more regular fashion, and new forms of social organisation have emerged. As Fligstein (2008) says, where people and organisations from different countries interact routinely, Europe-wide social fields emerge. As they are a part of those fields, European layers of identity can also be strengthened by this. However, an entrance to those fields is neither automatic nor available to all citizens. As we have already shown, a certain amount of economic, cognitive and social resources is crucial. These signify different backgrounds, life opportunities, aspirations and ambitions in an individual's life which can hardly be generalised over entire populations. Several programmes designed to increase exchanges of students and teachers encourage social transaction and offer opportunities to those trying to enter those fields. The most significant is the Erasmus programme, which created a system of credit transfers and established specific social networks. It was shown that by 2004, a million students had taken part in the programme (Fligstein 2008, p. 180). Students who go abroad have the opportunity to socialise with people living in foreign countries, to learn foreign languages and to gain additional opportunities to work abroad.

In order to comprehend the dynamics of identification with the European space, it's important to explore the interplay between social forces and individuals' negotiation of their position in social structure. Therefore, we will focus on the dynamics within European social fields. As Fligstein (2008) says, there are many European social fields in the political, economic and social spheres. The question is, if there are infinite social fields, is the notion more of a metaphor than a hard sociological concept (cf. Favell 2008, p. 499)? Accordingly, it seems to be important to define what social fields are becoming Europeanised. However, it is not our primary interest to define what social fields exist where in European transnational space, but to explore the internal dynamics of particular fields, power relations, and the circulation of transnational resources. In the following chapter, we will focus on scrutinising the transnational social field linked to the European bureaucratic elite.

5. European bureaucratic social fields

The term 'bureaucrat' is commonly known; it can hold many connotations, but in general it is a neutral definition of someone who is working within an institution of government. But, when attaching the prefix 'euro-', the word becomes misleading in a way. Since its emergence, the meaning of the term has varied significantly. It has been acknowledged that the meaning was once attached to civil servants of the EU, to political elites who work and act in Brussels as well as to a non-transparent system of power, which replaced democratic institutions; however, in all contexts, the notion describes the distance between ordinary citizens and the European polity (e.g. Georgakakis and Rowell 2013, p. 3). Who, then, are the Eurocrats, and why is this question important for this study? There are many different approaches to tackle the issue that range from studies of elites, perspectives of international relations, and institutionalisation to the socialisation of individuals into European administrative machinery (extensive review in Georgakakis and Rowell 2013, pp. 3–6). Recent, (and most inspiring) perspectives studied the European bureaucracy as a transnational example of the European bureaucratic field as explored by Pierre Bourdieu (e.g. collection of studies edited by Georgakakis and Rowell 2013). The important contribution of these studies is their breaking with the unified picture of 'Eurocrats'. It has been argued that building EU institutions as a social field allows to better define EU institutions, their internal dynamics and their relative location in the political system of the European Union (Geogakakis and Weisbein 2010, p. 100). Viewing Eurocrats as part of a social field is of great interest to our study, as it is primarily oriented towards the identification processes taking place within this specific social category. Of interest to us are individuals considered transnationals who regularly participate in the European (transnational) social sphere. Those identifications result from the active participation of individuals within certain social spaces, in combination with various constructions and perceptions of those spaces as well as complex developmental trajectories, rooted values and structural dispositions. Those individuals take part in social spaces or fields which exceed the institutional environment. They are able to use their skills and resources to reach their goals in various areas of their lives. When viewing the Eurocracy as an institutional bureaucratic field, many important actors can be observed, with varying amounts of various resources and permanency in the field. Georgakakis (2013, p. 228) associated the EU institutions with the field of Eurocracy as an arena for negotiation and competition, "one that is populated with actors and groups among whom the proximities and distances are less a function of their national and institutional affiliations than of the structure of the sociological capital and skills they have accumulated during their lives' trajectories."

This approach bears resemblance to Fligstein and McAdam's strategic actions fields. In order to briefly illustrate the field of Eurocracy in general, we rely on the Georgakakis's cartography models (2013, p. 229):

Figure 5:1: Adaptation of Georgakakis's cartography models of the field of Eurocracy

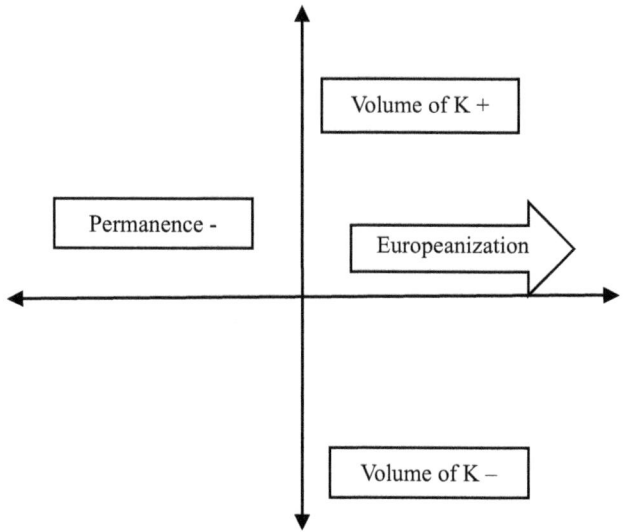

The vertical axis reflects a hierarchically ordered system, structured according to the overall amount of capital of all types that different groups of actors possess. As it is evident from the schema, between a director-general at the Commission and a counsellor at the permanent representation or a project coordinator of an NGO, the probability of exerting effects on the field differs. This disparity also relates to the nature of this capital, indicated by a horizontal axis (Georgakakis 2013, p. 229). Permanent actors in the field possess international social capital and thus have the authority they gained through their experience as insiders with responsibilities in their respective institutions. They are in a position that allows them to embody Europe or at least be perceived as a legitimate representative of common European interest. On the right side of the diagram are senior civil servants with long careers in European institutions. (ibid., p. 230). Our empirical implications for constructing instrumental and strategic identifications resemble that model, but there are some crucial differences. In our schema, the vertical axis represents social forces differentiated against one another. Actors more embedded in transnational social structures, connected to thin cultural influences, are more in the top, while actors wedded more to national social forces, tied to thick cultural influences, are more at the bottom. The position on transnational social structuring reflects the power one has in transnational social fields, which can overlap. The vertical axis shows transnational resources, including all types of transnational resources. The actors who possess more transnational resources are placed farther to the right, while actors with less transnational resources are farther to the left. The major difference between them lies in the nature of their resources, which aren't just linked to the institutional field. Transnational resources are understood in a broader sense, while in relation to the vertical axis, not only the position within the bureaucratic field is important, but also the distance from the national social environment. Our conclusions will allow us to understand the dynamics of identification within the specific area of the European institutional field, which represents itself in the European social spaces.

5.1. Fieldwork and analysis of ethnographic material

Our main focus is civil servants working in different departments and services of the European Commission, which is a highly bureaucratic institution with over 30,000 employees. The majority of the Commission staff is permanent, while almost one third of the Commission's current staff consists of officials hired on a temporary basis. The study focuses on officials who are called 'administratives of the European Union' and are involved in "a long-term process of constructing European social positions, closely linked to European institutions" (Georgakakis 2010, p. 140). European civil servants represent the group, who, compared to others employed there (for instance temporary agents), occupy a dominant position in terms of their number and their political power. Thus, they are distinctively different from other groups in the field. As Geograkakis (2013, p. 28) explains, they are one of the

> "rare groups within the European political system to have grown in number while securing permanent positions based on the production and accumulation of an EU institution-specific capital."

The study draws its conclusions from interviews, which were obtained during a period of ten months between September 2012 and April 2014. Some of the interviews were accompanied by an ethnographic study in Brussels, while the majority, due to lack of time, were obtained via Skype. It is to be noted that the ethnographic fieldwork has some weak points. The first issue is an unsystematic sampling of interlocutors. The potential interviewers were contacted based on a snow-ball method, which allowed to examine a limited group of civil servants. In the case of some interlocutors, it took a great deal of persuasion before they decided to take part in the study. As one of the informants figuratively explained: "We have been so often examined so far that sometimes I feel like we are lab rats". Those attitudes also might have affected the answers negatively. The majority of the informants also demanded a high level of anonymity. Accordingly, we only included particular statements important for the analysis and not the whole transcripts. Considering the number of all employees of the European Union bureaucracy, one may ask how many people should be targeted by the research. Our study comprises fifteen in-depth conversations conducted on a basis of a semi-structured questionnaire. However, it is not our attempt to homogenise the targeted group. Most interesting are individuals who share similar transnational social enablements and constraints of social structure. Further, the important assumption of the study is that certain conditions need to be fulfilled in order to enter the transnational social sphere the interviewees occupy. They all come from countries that became members of the European Union after 2004. In that period, the European Union saw its greatest growth, which also represented an administrative challenge. An interesting study on socialisation processes in the European institutional machinery reveals that, among 'the new stuff', the European Commission relies to a heavy degree on the earlier stages of socialisation, which leads to an expectation of a short learning curve for newly arriving staff, which isn't always realistic (e.g. Ban 2008). The interplay between national and transnational social forces could thus show itself in a specific manner. In order to fill the gap left by the ethnographic study, we also draw insights from some anthropological research studies on European bureaucratic elites (Abélès et al. 1993) and studies in which the narratives of those people were obtained (Ban 2008, 2009; Hooghe 2011; Georgakakis 2010). We used the material as secondary data analysed by a hermeneutic method.

5.2. Putting flesh on the bones

The ethnographic material was analysed based on open coding using the Atlas.ti qualitative analysis software. The analysis of the interview transcripts and participant observation field notes were conducted in three phases. The first one concerned the process of defining codes, which assign a summative, salient, essence-capturing attribute to a portion of data (Saldana 2009, p. 3). The main purpose of codifying is to arrange proposed notions into a systematic order, which can lead us to conclusions and potential paradigmatic models. The second phase, therefore, comprised the categorisation of codes into categories and code families. In the third phase, we engaged in the relational coding, in which we defined the contextual meaning of selected categories within a whole schema of qualitative study. The categorisation of codes turned out to be consistent with theoretical orientations.

The selected code families, which also present a common thread of the following analysis, are 'Predispositions influencing the entrance to the transnational social sphere', 'Transnational social forces', 'National social forces', 'Intersubjective meaning' and 'Instrumentality and strategic actions.' However, as we already emphasised, individual experiences should not be neglected. Narratives of interlocutors do form some common codes and code families, but a variety of personal backgrounds and aspirations are also important. Accordingly, extracts from individual experiences are represented in a separated part of the text. Those extracts reveal the unique processes of internal conversation and imagination, which can lead to analog life paths.

5.2.1. Predispositions influencing the entrance to the transnational social sphere

The narratives of interlocutors conveyed quite specific backgrounds, which led them to a position within the European institutional machinery. Firstly, there is an underlying theme of Europe as a country promised by former socialist countries. The discourses refer to new mythical horizons associated with Europe, which emerged in the years of when independent states were established after the collapse of communist regimes. These interviewees grew up in countries with a communist background. Accessing the European Union represented the 'return to Europe'. Working in European institutions was prestigious, as were the convergence with and integration into Europe. Also, the accession to the European Union became the prime objective of political efforts in transition countries. For instance, one of the interlocutors explained:

> "A desire to work in Brussels was present even before our country became a member of the European Union. I remember, when I was still in a high school, that when we talked about our future plans, you know, which faculty to choose, where to study, which occupation is the most appropriate, the most attractive jobs were abroad. And not just anywhere, but somewhere, where salaries are high, and where living standard is high, not like at home at that time. And because America is too far (laugh), European institutions sounded perfect. We imagined life there to be something special, much better than in our country. And once, I don't know, maybe in the third year, we went on the excursion to Brussels and Luxembourg with the school, and we saw all the beautiful expensive clothes, really fashionable, and cars, and everything was so neat."

However, entry to a transnational social sphere is not a given for every individual, and the option of adding a transnational layer to one's identities could be open to only a few. An individual's ability to access various types of resources plays an important role: social, economic and cultural. All informants were well equipped with several resources. The majority of them grew up in families endowed with supranational, cosmopolitan values. Travels across Europe or other continents were a matter of course, having regular contacts with other nationalities through friends, relatives or business partners was a part of everyday reality. As one of the informants said:

> "We moved to Canada, Ontario, when I was eighteen, because my mother got married again. I went to college there. I was a newcomer there and the easiest way to make friends was to bond with other foreigners. My best friend was from France. Together with my friends we formed a multicultural, multinational company."

They were encouraged to learn foreign languages and to gain knowledge in order to be successful someday. As one of the interlocutor expressed:

> "My parents always encouraged me to learn foreign languages. I also studied English and French and worked a part-time as a translator. And, you know, I always grabbed any opportunity to go abroad and to improve my language skills. And after joining the EU, all these institutions had a great need for translators, especially if you speak French. So, I started to work as a translator in Luxembourg first. And that was a beginning of the story."

We could say that all the respondents possessed a high amount of economic, social and cultural resources, but particular types of resources they possessed varied among them. For instance, one of the informants said that the financial status of her family was not high, but they still maintained regular contacts with family members living abroad. Broadening horizons was a value to them. Another informant said that his parents were quite rich and he had a chance to take language courses abroad every year. Their backgrounds are quite unique, but certain conditions were fulfilled. As one of the interlocutors said:

> "I grew up in a diaspora far away from a homeland. I was raised in a feeling that I should return someday. We had regular contacts with relatives and friends via Skype and Facebook and we travel a lot. Once, when I got back home for a visit, I got a chance to visit our expatriates in different part of Europe, also in Brussels. As I speak several languages, I got the opportunity to work in the European Parliament. Then, I obtained a degree in European affairs, and put some efforts to get a job in the Commission."

There is also a narrative that a home country did not offer enough opportunities to succeed and all of the informants were advised by their parents or close relatives that it is actually a must to get abroad. As one of the interlocutor said:

"Both of my parents are, let's say, intellectuals. They were always giving me a feeling that I should be good at school and that I must stand out from the average. All this because they wanted me to go abroad, and to finish schooling somewhere else. They always said, here you cannot succeed. I felt under pressure because of that. I even missed the trip with my school mates in the last year of the high school, because they wanted me to attend a language course in a New York. And then I went to Utrecht and finish my bachelor's there. In the first two years, I felt lonely and in a way separated from my friend back home. Then I finished my master's in London. And finally, I couldn't imagine going back again, I mean permanently. So I started to look for proper job opportunities."

Before they decided to work for the European Commission, their everyday lives were far from only being wedded to a national environment. By gaining employment in the European Commission, they were able to take advantage of the opportunities offered to them by freedom of movement in Europe as well as other opportunities offered by institutions of the European Union. However, the pre-dispositions do matter. The possession of various resources is essential as it allows the transition from local and national social fields to transnational ones. As Favell (2009, p. 65), who studied builders of the European society in the making, emphasised, "a rational movement can also be initiated by an opportunity arising at a particular moment that coincides with a lack of other constraints". Transnational (European) identifications are to a large extent marked not only by the participation in a transnational sphere but also by autonomous reflexivity, which is often a result of "contextual discontinuity" (cf. Archer 2003). The stories of the interlocutors not not only stress the role of the resources that allow entrance to transnational fields but also that of experiences that make their position in a social context uncomfortable.

Autonomous reflexives may not have formed extensive ties to a particular community (Archer 2003) or ties that were formed can become uncomfortable in a later phase of life. Individuals who experience contextual discontinuity are trying to uproot themselves by pursuing their projects and by solving potential clashes by prioritizing work. The narratives obtained reveal that due to different resources that influence social interactions, education, and opportunities to travel, the interlocutors were able to recognise the constraints of the national environment, which triggered internal conversation leading to deliberate reflexions. Thus, they were able to establish personal opinions oriented towards a transnational, multicultural environment that offered personal success and economic status. Based on concerns, projects and following practices (Archer 2003), they were able to accomplish concrete courses of action leading to employment in the transnational sphere, particularly in the field of Eurocracy.

5.2.2. Transnational social forces

Transnational social forces trigger individuals' internal conversation, but they also constitute the puzzles of habitus, which can be unconscious (unless they become contested and lead to a conscious deliberation, which we will demonstrate later). Institutional rules within particular European social fields ensue from the specific constitution of the EU, which defines the contents and limits of those rules by asserting a set of laws, norms and projects. The topography of networks relies on a systemic agenda that encourages the horizontal connectivity of individuals and groups on transnational and supranational levels. Semantics pertain to the mental organisation of the environment, which combines local, national and transnational social spheres, and thus convey significant transformations in structural order. All of the three social forces play a particular role in the social field of Eurocracy. There is interplay between institutional rules, cognitive frames, and networks, which influence the internalisation of institutional narratives. All informants provide similar thoughts about Europe as a common destiny, a post-national space, where individuals are building lives founded on human rights and universal values. It is a space of better living opportunities. They also define the European Union the same way. Their narrative reveals uniformed expressions about the political purposes, cultural influences and social dimensions of the Union. As one of the informants explained:

> "Europe is a continent where, according to geographical and cultural definitions to a certain extent, Europeans live … us. But, we employees, we try to tell what is the European Union, which is a different notion as a Europe. We (institutions) try to do our best for the Europe to work together, to be unified, and to prevent conflicts and wars. The EU is a political definition of states, which decided to cooperate with each other, to make more connected alliances, to share good practices in order to delegate a part of sovereignty to a common institutional formation. To reach the level where, instead each country makes decision of its own, we could work together."

Or, as another informant said:

> "The EU is a political institution, which advocates and defends the values of peace, democracy and freedom…ok, historically we know that the ruins of the Second World War contributed to the idea of peace and cooperation. But nowadays, I think it is especially a political power, which is important for the outside relations. Small countries, like Slovenia, but also France, Spain…in the world you don't have enough influence and only the EU can enable us to exercise our interests…in comparison to China, America. These is one aspect; the other is that it brings us together, it enables us certain ways of living, we can travel without passports, we can find jobs elsewhere."

Similar observations have already been noted by Wodak (2004), who conducted a discursive analysis based on interviews with civil servants and members of the European parliament. She determined that there were many similarities in the definitions of Europe given by all of the interviewed, who expressed shared beliefs tied to a shared past, present and future of Europe (ibid., p. 123). She also observed that the discourses on Europe resemble the themes relevant to the discursive construction of a nation as well as definitions of "out-groups", which turned out to be relevant in our study as well. As one of the informants expressed:

> "The first association, while you are in Europe, is that you hardly identify yourself as the European, usually you describe yourself as Polish or English or Slovenian, whatever, I think that you start to perceive and feel European when you are somewhere abroad. I mean, we are different from Asians, Americans. I see that Europe starts on this point. I think that when it comes to other continents, we can feel that we share the same values, social programmes, democracy and values of freedom."

The anthropological report on the European Commission (Abélès et al. 1993, p. 4) revealed that there is a kind of proper culture of Commission, a sense of shared concepts and values. *L'idee Europeenne* or the "European idea" is in the core of this culture. It has even been suggested that the relative consistency and clarity of the officials' ideas of "being European" act as a sort of "European conscience" (Cini 1996, in Wodak 2004, p. 123). By examining the social process of unification focusing on European civil servants' unions, Georgakakis (2006, p. 27) determined that the relation that connects and unites the body of Eurocrats with the EU institutions comes to pass through the proposition of its legal definitions and the various resources linked to it. The objectification of the European civil servants as a group is rooted in the institutional narratives of the European reality. The majority of European officials were educated in specialised European schools, a fact that is evident in the obtained interviews. During their education, they were already exposed to particular narratives defining Europe and European identity, which influenced their perception and motivation in choosing their work environment. One of the interlocutors emphasised the importance of a specific educational background. As she explained:

> "...I came here by accident, I hadn't studied European affairs before or anything related to that subject, and all people here had a lot of knowledge on the subject and were really skilful in their work. My background refers to communication studies, and I really felt that I don't belong here. But, in time they take you in."

The transfer of cultural and social information occurs also through specific exams, which they have to pass in order to get a job. The exams are specifically designed for particular groups within institutions. As the other informant similarly expressed:

"The majority of them (EU officials) studied European affairs before, then they passed the exam here after studying for one or two years, and immediately they become a part of Eurocrat machinery, they took that for granted."

Geogakakis (2013, p. 38) argues that EU civil servants form a sort of "status group" in the Weberian sense, which partly ensues from their permanency in the European institutional field, and is maintained by legal presentation that establishes and confirms its stability and durability as a principle. Furthermore, the evolution of that status group ensues from a set of social filters, which distinguish them from other agents (ibid.). European officials form a specific distanced group, and certain knowledge and skill (and time of acclimatisation to the group, and vice versa)are necessary to become a part of it. As one of the informants said:

"People working for the EU institutions are very specific. Firstly, they are all very intelligent, very ambitious, especially us, the new generation of the new members. But above all, they are all very bureaucratic. The old generation is actually completely cut off from the real world outside the EU institutions. From this perspective, it was very difficult to make contacts initially, because at the beginning, I didn't feel quite a part of this."

The majority of the interlocutors described the distance between EU officials and others regarding national environments. The majority of the EU administrative staff lived or worked abroad before, speaks various languages, and possesses post-graduate degrees. Furthermore, they are all very much committed to the European Union. As Hooghe (2011, p. 2) observes, these characteristics are not as common among national civil servants, national politicians or even among European citizens in general. During conversations with the informants, it has been often emphasised that, they don't talk about their work to friends when going back home for a visit. This relates to distance between them and others who are not employed in EU institutions. For instance, one said:

"Sometimes I talk about it with my father, but almost never with my friends. They are not even interested in it, and, let's say, I mention the European Parliament or European Commission, and some of them even don't know the difference."

The attachment and loyalty to the European Union increase with the years of affiliation with the EU institutions. Over time, the influence of transnational social forces becomes more visible. References to statements referring to the influence of integration in the European bureaucratic structure can also be found in the research conducted by Georgakakis and Weisbein (2010). In their examination of European commissioners and civil servants, they determined that the latter are increasingly committed to European institutions and the political agenda of united Europeans, while those who embody their authority (Commissioners) are less and less involved in this process. As they (2010, p. 140). observe:

> "Commissioners seem to be gaining in national political capital to the detriment of a professional commitment to EU politics. Conversely, the top-level officials increasingly appear to owe their positions to long-term investment in the EU institutions involving the production and simultaneously, the accumulation of specific European resources and skills."

In time, they also develop common supranational, 'European' values (Hooghe 2011), which pertain to the European Union as a shared source for political motivation. As one of the informants, who worked there for eight years, expressed:

> "For me personally, purely ideological, motivation comes from reasons for which the EU has been awarded for the Nobel Peace Prize. It's true that you can find here many different, contradicting interests, you can find Mafia or whatever, but you have this also at home. But here is everything on a higher level, a greater dimension. I believe in this idea and I am willing to fight for it. I am working for this his every day. As being a part of this institution, I can see the results."

The last expression also implies a sense of control over their lives and influence on social setting, which we take into account later in the chapter. The European Commission also shapes their lives by influencing social networks of EU officials. Commission employers have a special tax rate that applies to people living in certain areas. Accordingly, they live in a kind of ghetto, having their own sports clubs, their own crèches, and their own schools. They are in a certain way isolated from the rest of Brussels. Accordingly, all of the informants expressed quite strong feelings of attachment to the supranational political and social entity and of belonging to Europe as a whole. If we consider identifications as a marble cake of different layers, the European component is quite substantial. However, it is always complementary to a national counterpart.

5.2.3. National social forces

Searching for common values and close connections between EU officials and their identifications also leads us to the influence of national social forces. Although Eurocrats are actively participating in the European transnational social fields, they are also embedded in national ones. Among social forces, the crucial role is played by semantics of the social order. They represent a mental organisation of the social environment, which depends greatly on cultural containers that offer groundings for revaluating our position in society and supply orientation for our behaviour. The national layers of cognitive frames communicate stable and essential cultural meanings rooted in history and deeply embedded in a society's institutions and practices. Due to contemporary social transformations, culture took on different meanings of self-categorising and self-identifying, which signified essential semantic components substituting traditional conceptions of community, such as territory and history (Sassatelli 2010). The cognitive organisation of an environment can entail different levels of belonging, which are not physically defined but imagined. However, although Eurocrats are increasingly involved in their personal projects, relying heavily on their own resources, knowledge and skills, they are not immune to national social forces. In the online survey on European policy administration (e.g. Hooghe 2011), it has been shown that there is a considerable disagreement among those who believe that the EU should be supranational or intergovernmental.

These differences have their roots in the national backgrounds of respondents. Supranationalists are the programmatic descendants of Monnet, Hallstein, and presumingly also of Delors, and are moderately left-libertarian. It is argued that they predominantly come from small, decentralised, non-Protestant countries with a presumingly less effective government. State-centrists's perceptions and attitudes are closer to those of national politicians. In opposition to supranationalists, they predominantly come from large, centralised, Protestant countries. They are assumed to be former national civil-servants, working in polity areas that don't contain any technical content. Further they should be placed in the centre-right (Hooghe 2011, p. 19). Although they are all strongly committed to the European Union, they are also advocating their national interests while working in the European institutions. While talking about interest and motivations, they also express a discourse of "us and them", which pertains to their country of origin juxtaposed against other nation-states. As one interlocutor said, "If we won't help ourselves, the Germans won't do it either".

Their particular countries of origin are also associated with a homeland, and hold a strong connotation of home, a place where one can feel safe. In a narrative journey, the space that is the closest to home is most soothing and domestic, but it is not necessarily the space one inhabits. Accordingly, homes are also created and sustained by such narratives as: "this is where I come from, or my people come from" (Ahmed 1999, p. 346). Those images are sustained by regular contacts through social networks pertaining to a national environment, which remain strong. As one of the informants expressed:

> "Here I have a lot of friends, and we are socialising regularly. But, I still have friends back home, and those connections are still very tight. I feel great, when I come back and see my friends. In a way, I could even say that those friendships are stronger. Those relationships were established in primary school or even in a childhood. Here you just get to

know people, you're my friend and all, but maybe, at that age, when you meet people, you can't build such strong ties as in childhood."

The distance from 'home' and more regular participation in networks linked to the Commission environment can also be a source of anxiety. The narratives of the majority of interlocutors conveyed the sort of disunity linked to their private life. They prefer living in multicultural, multi-lingual environments. They raise their children in cosmopolitan spirit, but can feel uncomfortable with that. The influence of thick cultural information and memory can be quite obvious in the otherwise cosmopolitan Brussels. One can notice that each national group has established its own club, encouraged the existence of a network, which they carefully maintain, as well as its own association of European civil servants. Some of them even have a church (also e.g. Abélès et al. 1993). However, not all officials feel a need to socialise with their own countrymen and, further, they do not necessarily feel anxious about it. As one of the informants expressed:

"It's true that we are mostly connected with people working in the institutions, and we are often isolated from the local environment and from our relatives especially, but if you put in some efforts, it is not necessarily a case. Usually, we are so busy that there's no time to go out anyway (laugh)."

There are also other situations, in which national social forces come to the fore. European institutions are multinational, culturally diverse and multilingual social environments. To speak one official language and to regularly shift to another is an efficient and persistent sign of the diversity and variety of national traditions, narratives, cultural backgrounds and histories (Shore 2004). As Abélès et al. (1993, pp. 38–41) determined, the collision of a variety of national characteristics can reinforce particular stereotypes like north versus south, French- versus English-speakers, and so on. National cultural memory is based on thick cultural influences, which are deeply rooted in an individuals' perception of the social world and cannot just simply disappear in a multicultural, multilingual environment. But the situation can also be reversed. In contrast, the traditional narratives of national differences are in some occasion even promoted by the Commission itself which is evident from some features of the modes of recruitment and promotion, by the cabinets system, and the ENDS (the *experts nationaux detaches*). These aspects create fundamental contradictions in the very core of the organization (ibid., p. 41). European institutions are a conglomerate of national diversities, which are contrasted against each other on a daily basis, and thus become even more visible on certain occasions. For instance, according to one interlocutor:

"There are special working dynamics, you have to communicate with people in a different manner and cultural differences often come to the fore. You have to be careful how you interact with others. Maybe you have to be a little more aware of your behaviour as if you work in national environment, where you know the cultural framework. If you make a joke, maybe you won't be funny but stupid."

However, those differences are predominantly perceived as an asset. The tensions created by the ambiguity of identification and by constantly being reminded of so many 'others' are a part of the multicultural atmosphere of the Commission. As was stated in a survey conducted by Abélès et al. (1993), there is a strong and prevailing belief amongst many officials in the Commission that European civil servants have managed to overcome all those national stereotypes. "There is 'an *esprit europeen*' and a European identity. If differences exist, they refer to varieties of personalities and characters, and not to the group as a whole. Accordingly, if cultural differences can be noticed, they accord to the 'Europe's richness'" (ibid., p. 39). It is also evident that defending national interest is often seen as linked to a common European prosperity, which reflects the influence of transnational social forces rather than of national ones. The prosperity of one's own country is thus not possible without the prosperity of the European Union as a whole. As one of the interlocutors said:

"It is of our great interest that the European Union exists and that we all cooperate together. To fight for the common good and for the united Europe and Europeans actually means fighting for your own country."

5.2.4. Intersubjective meaning

As we have already mentioned, practical logic, which leads to articulations of dispositions, positions, and figurations, always proceed through intersubjective meaning-making. It is of great importance how people interact with each other and with whom they interact. As Georgakakis (2006) postulates, understanding the relations among European officials allows better understanding of how their identities contribute to the construction of the standards that build and constitute European politics as a whole and provides them their relative coherence. It is not just the influence of transnational social forces as such, but the transfer of meanings through intersubjective practice.

In that sense, the Eurocracy can be seen as a strategic action field, where there is a tension between 'incumbents' and 'challengers' (Fligstein and McAdam 2012, pp. 10–13). Incumbents are the actors who possess the most power within a field. Their interests are also heavily represented in the prevailing mode of organisation of the strategic action field. The social settings and common goals of the field are adapted to their interests. Challengers occupy less privileged positions. However, if they recognise and comprehend the nature of the field and the prevailing rules of the game of incumbent actors, they can propose their own visions for the field and their position in structural settings. Georgakakis (2010, p. 97) emphasises that internal struggles and the whole dynamics of working processes in EU institutions are sectorally or nationally grounded. But, those struggles are also anchored in the social, professional or academic background of people working in those institutions. Furthermore, power relations and domination play an important role, as they are linked to the amount of resources related to their position, where it is crucial to recognise the symbolic hierarchy of their title and former background (ibid., p. 97).

In the field of Eurocracy, there are many different actors, and that contributes to complex dynamics of intersubjective meaning-making and thus also influences the substance and intensity of particular identity layers. A great difference between established employees and newcomers starting after 2004 can be observed. The interviewees are part of the second group. They all experienced a great disparity between 'them and us'. They share a feeling and a need to prove they are worthy of their position in the institution. One can notice a kind of respect towards the older generation, but one can also find a sort of condescending attitude among new officials. In the eyes of the interlocutors, they are seen as being detached from reality, overwhelmed with illusory ideas about the EU. The younger generation is driven by different motivation stimuli.

As the study on work motivation among European officials reveals (cf. Ban and Vandenabeele 2009), some conventional and often articulated narratives are reproduced by many within the Commission itself that say the early pioneers were really committed to build up Europe, while those who started work in later years are increasingly considered career builders. In that regard, they presumingly do neither have the same kind of passion for their work nor loyalty for the institution. It's important to note that the majority of so called newcomers is more motivated by the challenges and new enablements of the work. Their eagerness is also encouraged by an interest in advancing their work on specific policy issues and thus bringing it to a new level (Ban and Vandenabeele 2009). They want to surpass their predecessors, which is evident in their struggle to identify themselves which permeates organisational and personal layers of their identity marble cake alike. The articulation of figurational relations (Mouzelis 2007) and intersubjective meaning-making is also linked to the internal structure of the European Commission, which we were not able to detect in our own ethnographic study.

As Abélès et al. (1993, pp. 4–5) discovered, in the European Commission, a whole complex of ideas, concepts and values exists, which determines both the discourse and conduct of officials and the relationship between them. The sense of sharing all these values leads to a common identity or a strong organisational identity, but the latter also coincides with compartmentalisation. An individual official can simultaneously perceive himself or herself as being a part of the organisation as a whole or as being a part of a smaller group (Directorate Generale – DG). "The perceived layering of identities here might seem to guarantee the Commission's own 'cultural cohesion'" (ibid., p. 5). There is an internal struggle and a specific dynamic between different departments, which significantly influences officials' identifications, contexts of belonging, and their access to information. Consequently, internal struggles also influence the ability of individuals to obtain resources, which are crucial for their strategic actions. However, the latter also has a certain influence on transnational identifications. Referencing Abele et al. (1993, p. 33) again, it is obvious that small departments can construct a self-conscious micro-identity that reaches beyond national particularities and differences:

> "We share the same references, we speak the same language'. Or, as one official said, 'We have known cases of disputes arising from linguistic and cultural misunderstandings, not so much within a department but between departments and with outsiders."

5.2.5. Instrumentality and strategic action

Thus far, our analysis examined the interlocutors' articulation of their respective position in relation to a number of social forces that range from transnational to national levels with regard to each other's behaviour. It reveals the unconscious puzzles of habitus and deliberate decisions resulting from internal conversations. They proceed to employ the practical logic that leads to their actions and identifications, which are very much instrumental and strategic. In this regard, habitus is a subject of deliberation at the unconscious level,, while reflexivity increases. The examined Eurocrats are not just bureaucratic personnel working in institutions of the European Union. They are also transnationals who build their life-stories using a variety of social spheres. They are not wedded only to the national environment, but they are actively participating in a transnational one, and thus reproduce different social contexts. as they are quite well equipped with several resources, they are able to take full advantage of European citizenship. Firstly, to a degree they are free from national environment. They all share the opinion that they wouldn't be able to do as well in their home countries. As one of the informants expressed:

"The situation here is much different, when comparing it to my colleagues working in public administration at home. Here, the key difference lies in the fact that I have a feeling of being treated seriously. I'm treated the same as Germans, French, Spaniards… Here, it really does not matter where you are from. It counts only to have good ideas and to know how to realise it. There are too many people, and the stress is on their abilities. I feel equal here, I can move forward. If you are good and successful, you can succeed."

They are motivated not only by good salaries also by personal fulfilment. They want to be successful and be evaluated accurately. The majority of interlocutors said that perhaps someday they will return to their nation of origin, but this will be a deliberate decision, and not a necessity. They broadcast a sense of superiority, which is linked to their awareness of agential possibilities and possibilities to control their own life. Their decision to take a job in the European bureaucratic machinery was a deliberate and individualistic one, reflecting a high level of reflexivity. Using Favell's (2008, p. 63) statement, we can say "and calculation is still ongoing". Some of them said they are under a lot of pressure in their work environment and have a really stressful life, but this is something they enjoy and want. As one of the interlocutors said:

"Sometimes it gets really hard. But I like it. When I'll have enough, I will go somewhere else. Maybe I will start with my own business or maybe I'll take some other less stressful position in the EU."

In a world of unstable and unpredictable social conditions, they are very skilful when it comes to taking risk according to Beck's (1992) risk society. They know how to take advantage of institutional rules to create a safe environment for themselves. They are distanced from other European citizens, and have independent imaginations and aspirations. They aim for high goals and are aware of the spectrum of opportunities they can make use of. They are well-educated and resourceful individuals, who are trying to get the best out of their situation. They possess notable social skills, which allow them to attain collective action and give meaning and sense to their lives (cf. Fligstein and McAdam 2012, p. 46). They travel a lot and move through a range of social contexts. They evaluate the situation in their native society from a different economic, political and social perspective. Some of them explicitly express that they feel capable of influencing national situations. The transition between fields enables more intensive reflexivity and consideration of one's action and of the institutional frames in which they are embedded. They perceive themselves as contributors to their social conditions.

Living beyond national society, they have established new lives in Brussels, which offer a specific transnational or even supranational environment. In that social environment, they have created multi-layered, changeable identities, heavily emphasising the European component as it's their source of connectivity. It brings all these people coming from different national societies together, and they are aware of it. Their predominant values are linked to diversity and travelling. They see not just Europe, but also the world as interconnected spaces. Furthermore, they attempt to impart those values to their children. More than half of the interlocutors already have a family or intended to have one in the near future. They create families that undermine the patterns of traditional communities and homes. This not only shapes their specific social field but the stories of everyday life linked to a new European society in the making (Favell 2008). Their children are growing up in a specific multilingual, multicultural, multinational environment. They are socialising with peers who have different ethnic and linguistic backgrounds from their own. For instance, one of the informants is married to a woman with a mixed ethnic background. They have two children and at home they speak three languages excluding English, which they learn in school. As he said:

> "Sometimes it gets very interesting at home, quite Babylonian, but we are all well accustomed to this arrangement. I have to say that children are much more responsive to such situations than we adults."

As previously mentioned, transnational (European) identifications ties people together who share them. Transnational layers of identities thus take on instrumental meanings and allow individuals to have greater control over their lives and to more easily achieve their goals. This shows how constant border crossing (physical or imaginary), transnational social interaction and institution, and personal experiences from the past and other national or local environments create the perception of the present and also of the self. They can easily switch among different layers of identities which they are aware of.

In the analysis, it turned out that their social practices also lead to identifications and expression of a sort of transnational habitus, which is to a large extent influenced by transnational social forces. They all form a strong organisational identity, and they embody European interests as narrated by the Commission. Their European layer of identity is embedded in these narrations. However, although the influence of transnational social forces is not always conscious, when it comes into conflict with their interests, reflexivity is strongly employed. Here, habitus as we understand it comes to light. In the field of Eurocracy, the interlocutors gained new puzzles of habitus and thus added new dimensions to their set of dispositions, making it possible for them to reorient their imaginations and actions. However, those dimensions can also trigger internal conversation, if the social context is not linked to their interests in a particular field. The embodiment of certain institutional values and official narratives helps them to consolidate their position within the field, and it serves their interests and needs. They are committed to the European Union and consequently they feel to be Europeans themselves, but in specific social contexts they can distance themselves from 'Europeaness'. As one of the interlocutors said:

> "I know I'm a part of the Eurocrat bubble. But it is important not to lose the link with the other part of the word. That's why I always keep one leg outside (laugh)."

They are simultaneously inserted into European bureaucratic machinery and at the same time capable of maintaining a distance towards it. As we have shown, transnational social forces have an impact on their narratives about Europe, the European Union, and their position in it. However, when it is necessary, they can opt out of it. Those narratives represent the influence of thin cultural frames, which are not durable or essential, but more individualistic, and especially rational. As one of the informants said:

> "I feel like an European, but what is most important is that the EU enables certain things such as going abroad, to take a job elsewhere. It makes our lives easier."

Their identification with European space exceeds the boundaries of the institutional environment. The more transnational (European) resources they possess and the more they are embedded in transnational structural composition, the more they are able to control their life-paths. Their European identifications are not only instrumental considering figurational relations within a field, but also when conducting additional life projects linked to their personal, family or career paths outside the European commission. Within the field of Eurocracy, their "logic of practice" expresses the rules of the game and "know how" within it (cf. Bourdieu 1990). However, we should not to forget that their internal conversation reflects their presence in multiple social fields, national and transnational, linked to social networks crossing different social categories and spaces, where they can use their transnational social skills according to their transnational resources. Their identifications with the European Union and wider European space are highly substantiated by institutional imperatives, but also reach beyond the boundaries of institutions. Transnational and national social forces in particular fields are complex and dispersed. Those individuals possess a lot of transnational resources, European not just as part of an institution but also in terms of social networks, information and knowledge linked to a broader European space and other social fields. They are not just highly reflexive when it comes to defining their goals and identifications. They can also make post-reflexive choices. In this regard, one may find important the idea of relational reflexivity, proposed by Archer (2012, p. 55), who says that emergent powers of social structure operate according to "any end, however inchoate, that can be intentionally entertained by human beings". Therefore, social settings condition individuals' ability to act, seeing that this interplay "works through shaping the situations – from the accessibility of resources to the prevalence of beliefs – in which agents find themselves" (ibid., p. 55). In that way, some actions can be discouraged, others encouraged (ibid., p. 55). In that sense, the interplay between habit and action should be considered through the lens of perspective, always treating socialisation as a matter of relations.

However, the availability of resources is crucial in recognising the enablements or constraints of social contexts. For Eurocrats, the influence of transnational (institutional) social forces sometimes works unconsciously, and in some other occasions can turn into a subject of deliberate decision. They have triggers to their disposal that enable them to form supranational instrumental identifications, while individuals limited to national social spheres are deprived of them. In proposing that one who is wedded only to a national sphere can orient his or her prospects to living in a transnational sphere (which means that he or she possesses some of the necessary resources or capital that allow him to recognize enablements of living in a supranational sphere, but the amount of them is not sufficient), his ability to make post-reflexive choices is not self-evident. Eurocrats have the ability to imagine and reflexively deliberate concerns and transfer them into projects as they have the ability to make post-reflexive choices in that regard.

The experiences of one interlocutor can clearly demonstrate this. He worked as a civil servant for many years, then he decided to go back to his country, but still worked for the European Commission. He employs a narrative of defending national interest, which he perceives himself to be able to do due to his position in the field and all the resources he possesses. However, it would be incorrect to say that he realised his decision, because national social forces prevail over transnational ones, and his aspirations were linked to defending national interests. His decision is predominantly a personal one, as he wants to live together with a partner who cannot afford to move to Brussels. His position in the institutional field enables him to take control over his life. Moving back to his homeland does not mean stepping out of the transnational environment, as his occupation is still linked to the Eurocracy. He is capable of conducting his life by switching between different cultural repertoires and instrumentally adapting his personal, organisational, national and transnational identifications according to social context.

European bureaucrats seem to be constantly on the move, capable of recreating their economic, political, social, and cultural incorporation in the societies they live in. Their social practices convey the simultaneous presence of two places as well as constant movement across borders while creating certain social memories, discourses and feelings of belonging. Thus, they create a specific marble cake of identifications tied to European and national social environments. Their identities, behaviour and values are not limited by location. They construct and deploy flexible personal, national and transnational identities. Eurocrats form layers of identities that draw from and at the same time contest and oppose national identities. The concept of thetransnational social field is capable of shedding light on the dynamics of identity constructions, which in the transnational sphere are more specific. Actions of individuals in the social field of Eurocracy are influenced by specific combinations of national and transnational social forces and are influencing them vice versa. The important fact is that they are capable of revaluating their position in the social structural composition and of orienting their action towards better life opportunities. They are able to cross national boundaries and strategically create new lives in a transnational social sphere. They cannot escape from social constraints but their deliberate and strategic actions turn those into enablements offered by the social environment. The narratives of the interlocutors reveal important dynamics of identifications within the social fields; however, each component of the meaning-making within the social game (Bourdieu 1977) deserves thoughtful consideration and could serve as a topic itself. This study represents a framework for future research focusing on power relations between incumbents and challengers, transnational social forces creating new European social structures, as well as changed transnational practices and social connections.

6. Conclusion

This chapter will present final conclusions of the research, whereas the aims of the study were, hopefully, achieved. The first goal of the book was to explore identifications in a contemporary world, while considering the role of the increasing global flows of ideas, popular culture, money and employment that coincide with changes in communication technologies in the transformation of the traditional, positional views on identity. Based on critical evaluations of the existing theories and studies, we sketched the theoretical model of identifications that is implied on a transnational sphere. In order to capture the complex relation between human agency and social structure, we drew from the theory of social fields, transferred to the transnational level. The model considers social practices occurring in the interplay between national and transnational social forces and individuals' deliberations of their position in social context. While taking into account the accelerated reflexivity as well as the consciously deliberated dimensions of habitus significant for the transnational social environment, we proposed that identifications are strategic and instrumental.

The theoretical assumptions and potential empirical implications were further applied to the issue of identification with the European space. We treated the European Union as a specific form of a transnational political and social entity composed of different social fields. Following our theoretical framework, we theoretically and empirically represented the role of everyday practices and activities on the supranational level, pre-dispositions in entering the European social fields, and the influence of each type of social forces. A special emphasis was put on semantics as a self-referential organisation of the social environment, which present a crucial ingredient to define a self. Humans' semantics express the role of cultural information and memory, which enable the formation of a distinct social group. According to our previous theoretical and partly empirical endeavour, cultural information or memory was supposed to be more thin and prone to transformation. We evaluated the meaning of the European transnational social fields by using a qualitative research strategy, that enabled us to explain the role of social forces, situated intersubjectivity and internal conversation by drawing its insight from narratives. We thus managed to represent the potential of a theory of transnational social fields in the exploration of contemporary identifications, which are more consciously and reflexively constructed, in a comprehensive manner.

However, there are still many open issues connected to the interplay between social forces and human agency leading to strategic identifications. Although the European Union has existed for several decades, the patterns of intra-migration and consequences of participation in a transnational social sphere are a subject that should attract scholarly intention in the future. European social spaces represent European society in the making. It is difficult to predict what will happen in following years and decades. One should not neglect that while the European institutional and political situation enabled transnational participation and identification, it has also become obvious that the future of European integration was seriously questioned after the recent economic crisis. This is not merely a financial or economic crisis as it reflects the insufficiency of the institutional order and the system of government, which otherwise could mitigate and limit the consequences of the crisis and resolve its causes. The crisis is therefore also a political one that undermines the legitimacy of existing political environments on local, national and supranational levels. It has even become questionable if the EU will be able to survive as a recognizable entity (Giddens 2012). The financial turmoil calls for a new fiscal and monetary policy, but this requires a different institutional organization and political integration. The crisis seems to limit opportunities to interact across borders and pressures people to stay within national boundaries. European layers of identifications as elements of a marble cake are thus less intensive and leave space for other layers, which are more restricted to local or national environments. There is also another dimension that should not be neglected. Economic prosperity alone is certainly not a sufficient factor to create identifications with the EU but it is an important condition. Neil Fligstein (2008, p. 2) showed how the proliferation of markets and economic growth induced the existence of economic, social and political fields across Europe, which led to an increasing number and density of social interaction across Europe's national borders. This encouraged the willingness of people to identify as Europeans. The economic crisis has a negative effect on structures that enable social interactions and thus curtails the transaction of cultural information within cognitive frames.

The individuals who are able to participate in the transnational European sphere are thus far a minority. The question about the future of their descendants remains unanswered. In the case of our interlocutors, their children are far too young to be included in a comprehensive research. They are growing up in a social environment that is unique, multilingual, and cosmopolitan. Will they gro into the elite at the top of European society, or will they gradually become a mainstream society of the future European Union? There are also some open questions referring to the European integration in a political and economic sense. Again, thick and thin cultural influences play a part here, which are important especially considering the influence of national environments. The process of 'thinning' of cultural frames is far from being straightforward, and again raises the question of whether it is really inevitable or at least how fast it is proceeding. As these are topics worth being explored in greater detail, we leave them open. An important contribution of the study, which was theoretically and empirically revaluated and can represent a framework for further exploration, is the presumption that individuals in the modern world participate in many social fields that do not always correlate with local or national boundaries. Global processes enable the existence of transnational social fields, which forces us to re-examine and reconceptualise the relationship between imagined social spaces and physical places (e.g. Gargano 2009, p. 334). Drawing from this concept prevents us from limited considerations of "how spaces, identities, or networks of association are created or negotiated" (Gargano 2009, p. 335), but enables us to recognise a variety of struggles, power dynamics and consequences that appear as the outcome of individuals' encounters. Those individuals are coming from different social and cultural contexts, which make those encounters specific.

One should consider that an individual's meaning-making about the self and others, which leads to identifications, is far from straightforward. On the one side, there are structural forces and on the other, individuals. Social structure and individuals present emergent entities, which should not be equated. Social structures, entities or systems cannot exist without people; however, they cannot interfere with each other's projects directly. Our analysis reveals the role of European (transnational) habitus, which can unconsciously orient someone's imagination and behaviour; it can also present dispositions triggering inner conversations through which individuals are able to recognise enablements or constraint of social structure. The European habitus presents a puzzle of different dispositions gained in different social context on different spatial level, and is therefore local, national and transnational. Drawing upon Bourdieu, Luis Guarnizo (1998), for instance, proposed the idea of habitus as a transnational form "whereby practices and social positions that spread across borders produce conscious and non-conscious dispositions to act in specific ways in specific situations" (cited in Vertovec 2001, p. 26). A transnational habitus is constituted by "dispositions emerging from different local and national environments, and reflects a different context of a structured framework of evaluations and expectations which", as proposed by Bourdieu, "lead to the conscious or intuitive prioritising of certain dispositions and practices" (Kelly and Lusis 2006, p. 833). In that regard, habitus in regard to transnational social fields implies a meaning that is different from that we originally asserted, as it is more defined by movement between places, which allows more reflexive considerations of an individual's action within structured positions. In our consideration, the European habitus (or every habitus) presents not just conscious and non-conscious dispositions gained in different social positions in national and European level, but a disposition that can be conscious on certain occasions and non-conscious on others. Each part of the habitus-puzzle can be potentially deliberated through internal conversation, but certain conditions need to be fulfilled regarding possession of resources, which we explained above. Participation in transnational fields enables new fragments constituting the puzzle, which make those that are gained by involuntary agential position (via birth) less significant. Prepositions linked to a transnational social sphere are (even) more prone to trigger internal conversation and thus to induce deliberate reflexions.

Two things, therefore, seem to be important in combining reflexivity and habitus in relation to someone's social position and her or his actions. Non-conscious or semi-conscious dispositions that substantiate our responses to social situations and our social actions can be merged into conscious reflexions ensuing from the internal conversation provided we have enough resources on our disposal. Those resources enable us to recognise the constraints and enablements acting as potential causal powers of social structures. The resources entail a selection of different resources (economic, social, cultural, and human). Late modernity offers the mass dissemination of information, which makes more regular reflexivity possible. Furthermore, the unstable social situation (or risk society) forces us to be mobile in different contexts and thus to aquire new experiences and to add new dimensions to our set of dispositions. This leads us to the second important argument, that new dimensions of the habitus-puzzle (which are acquired over the course of social life and not ascribed during childhood) induce social discontinuity, which increases reflexivity. Those new dimensions can also work as unconscious dispositions in our imaginings but regularly turn conscious.

Regarding our study, we inferred the interplay between conscious and unconscious responses of social settings into the transnational social sphere and showed that possibilities for reflexivity are indeed present, and that European layers of identifications are to a large extent strategic and instrumental. The European habitus thus asserts a context of social and cultural information that individuals acquire in the European (transnational) sphere. As European identifications are always complementary to local or national ones, the European habitus can be seen as a complementary puzzle of multiple sets of dispositions, which create contested meanings and thus even encourage reflexivity. Deliberating on multiple, ambivalent social and cultural information contributes to the personal revaluation of social embeddedness of individuals. Through inner conversation, individuals mediate social structure in a way that evokes the enablements of social or cultural properties. In a transnational social sphere, the individuals represented in the book found opportunities to mediate upon enablements, while a national sphere is more constrained. Their concerns are oriented towards creating better life opportunities and identifications with the European space as part of their strategies. As those individuals have differing backgrounds, their marble cake of identity differs as well. The European puzzle of habitus may be the same (although there are different opportunities for members of different states) but the other parts of habitus are quite different. Therefore, in order to understand European identification, the set of dispositions and a variety of cultural information are important.

Instrumental identifications can be considered a result of deliberate reflexions, and unconscious dimensions of habitus play a negligible role. However, as identifications are always constructed or acquired within a certain social environment, social context is important. Accordingly, (transnational) social fields are able to offer this context as they allow concrete research on the way particular individuals and groups engage in interplay with concrete social forces. The concept of the transnational social field is capable of shedding light on the dynamics of identity construction which in the transnational sphere are more specific. Entry to a transnational social sphere is not a given for every individual, and adding a transnational layer to collective identities could be seen more as a privileged dimension of a few. An individual's ability to access various types of resources is important: social, economic and cultural. The possession of a selection of resources is essential as it opens the gate from local and national social fields to transnational ones. The transition between particular fields enables more intensive reflexivity and a consideration of an individual's action as well as the institutional frames in which they are embedded. Accordingly, transnational individuals have more social skills, which reflects what people do to attain collective action and give meaning and sense to their lives (cf. Fligstein and McAdam 2012, p. 46). Transnational layers of identity can thus take on instrumental meanings and allow individuals to have greater control over their lives and achieve their goals more easily. Furthermore, the concept of transnational social fields allows an understanding of the transnational context of the different dimensions of social fields in relation to cognitive frames, institutional rules and relational topographies of networks (Beckert 2010). It reveals how constant border crossing (physical or imaginary), transnational social interaction and institutions, and the past life experiences of an individual and from other national or local environments help them make sense of the present and the self.

7. List of references

Abélès, Marc / Bellier, Irene / Mcdonald, Maryon: *An Anthropological Approach to the European Commission. Report for the European Commission.* 1993. Retrieved 14.4.2015, from https://hal.archives-ouvertes.fr/halshs-00467768/document.

Adam, Frane / Makarovič, Matej / Rončević Borut / Tomšič Matevž: *The challenges of sustained development: the role of socio-cultural factors in East-Central Europe.* New York; Budapest: Central European University Press. 2005.

Ahmed, Sara: "Home and away: Narratives of migration and estrangement". *International Journal of Cultural Studies* 2 (3), 1999, pp. 329–347.

Akram, Sadiya / Hogan Anthony: "On reflexivity and the conduct of the self in everyday life: reflections on Bourdieu and Archer". *The British Journal of Sociology* 66 (4), 2015, pp. 605–626.

Adams, Mathew: "Hybridizing Habitus and Reflexivity: Towards an Understanding of Contemporary Identity?" *Sociology.* 40 (3), 2006, pp. 511–528.

Adler, Rachel: "Human agency in international migration: The maintenance of transnational social fields by Yucatecan migrants in southwestern city". *Mexican studies* 16, 2000, pp. 165–187.

Anderson, Benedict: *Imagined communities: reflections on the origin and spread of nationalism.* London: Verso. 1983.

Appadurai, Arjun: *Modernity at Large: Cultural Dimensions of Globalization.* Minneapolis: University of Minnesota Press. 1996.

Archer, Margaret: *Culture and agency.* Cambridge, New York, Cambridge University Press. 1988.

Archer, Margaret: *Structure, Agency, and the Internal Conversation.* Cambridge, New York, Cambridge University Press. 2003.

Archer, Margaret. *Making Our Way Through the World.* Cambridge: Cambridge University Press. 2007.

Archer, Margaret: *The Reflexive Imperative in Late Modernity.* Cambridge: Cambridge University Press. 2012.

Assman, Jan: "Collective memory and cultural identity". *New German Critique*, No. 65, Cultural History/Cultural Studies. Spring - Summer, 1995, pp. 125–133.

Bagnoli, Anna: "Between outcast and outsider: constructing the identity of the foreigner." *European Societies* 9 (1), 2007, pp. 23–44.

Ban, Carolyn: "The Making of the New Eurocrats: Self-Selection, Selection, and Socialization of European Commission Staff from the New Member States." *Paper prepared for conference l'Europe: Objet, agent et enjeu de socialisation*

Ecole Normale Supérieure, Lettres et Sciences Humaines, Lyon, France. 2008. Retrieved 16.5.2014, from http://uaces.org/documents/papers/0801/2008_Ban.pdf.

Ban, Carolyn / Vandenabeele, Wouter: "Motivation and values of European commission staff". *Paper presented at the European Union Studies Association meeting Marina del Rey, California*. 2009. Retrieved 16.5.2014, from:http://aei.pitt.edu/33022/1/Ban._Carolyn.pdf.

Basch, Linda / Glick Schiller, Nina / Blanc-Szanton, Christina (eds): *Nations Unbound: Transnational Projects, Postcolonial Predicaments, and Deterritorialized Nation-states*. Langhorn: Gordon and Breach. 1994.

Beck, Ulrich: *Risk Society. Towards a New Modernity*. London: Sage. 1992.

Beck, Ulrich / Giddens Anthony / Lash Scott: *Reflexive Modernization. Politics, Tradition and Aesthetics in the Modern Social Order*. Stanford, California: Stanford University Press. 1994.

Beckert Jens: "How Do Fields Change? The Interrelations of Institutions, Networks, and Cognition in the Dynamics of Markets". *Organization Studies* 31 (5), 2010, pp. 605–627.

Boer Den Pim / Bugge Peter / Waever Ole / Wilson Kevin / van der Dusses W J: *The History of the Idea of Europe (Book 1)*. London and New York: Routledge. 1995.

Buecker Nicola: "Returning to where? Images of 'Europe' and support for the processof EU integration in Poland". In Pawel I. Karolewski, Viktoria Kaina V. (eds.): *European Identity – Theoretical Perspectives and Empirical insights*. Berlin: Lit Verlag, 2006, pp. 265–295.

Burgess J. Peter: "What's so European about the European Union? Legitimacy between Institution and Identity". *European Journal of Social Theory* 5(4), 2002, pp. 467–481.

Bottero, Wendy: "Intersubjectivity and Bourdieusian approaches to 'identity'". *Cultural Sociology*, 4 (1), 2010, pp. 3–22.

Bourdieu Pierre: *Outline of a Theory of Practice*. Cambridge: Cambridge University Press. 1977.

Bourdieu Pierre: *The Logic of Practice*. Stanford, CA: Stanford University Press. 1990.

Bourdieu Pierre / Wacquant Loïc: *An Invitation to Reflexive Sociology*. Cambridge: Polity Press. 1992.

Bühlmann, Felix / Thomas David / André Mach: "Cosmopolitan Capital and the Internationalization of the Field of Business Elites: Evidence from the Swiss Case". *Cultural Sociology* 7 (2), 2011, pp. 211–229.

Brannen Julia / Nilsen Ann: "Individualisation, choice and structure: a discussion of current trends in sociological analysis". *The Sociological Review* 533, 2005, pp. 412–428.

Caetano, Anna: "Defining personal reflexivity: A critical reading of Archer's Approach". *European Journal of Social Theory*, 1–16, 2014, DOI: 10.1177/1368431014549684.

Checkel Jeffrey T. / Katzenstein, Peter: *European Identity*. Cambridge: Cambridge University Press. 2009.

Cohen, Erez: "I am my own culture: The 'individual migrant' and the 'migrant community', a Latin American case study in Australia". *Journal of Intercultural Studies* 25(2), 2004, pp. 123–142.

Davies Norman: *Europe: A History*. New York; Oxford University Press. 1996.

Delanty, Gerard: *Modernity and postmodernity: Knowledge, power and the self.* London; Thousand Oaks; New Delhi: Sage. 2000.

Delanty Gerard / Rumford, Chris: *Rethinking Europe. Social Theory and the Implications of Europeanization*. London and New York: Routledge. 2005.

Diez Medrano, Juan: "Europeanization and the Emergence of a European Society". *IBEI Working Papers*. 2008. Retrieved 16.6.2013, from http://www.recercat.net/bitstream/ha-dle/2072/4914/WP_IBEI_12.pdf%20accesat%20la%201?sequence=1.

DiMaggio, J. Paul / Powell. Walter W.: "The Iron Cage Revisited: Institutional Isomorphism and Collective Rationality in Organizational Fields". *American Sociological Review* 48 (2), 1983, pp. 147–160.

DiMaggio, J. Paul / Powell. Walter W.: (1991) "Introduction". In: Walter W. Powell, Paul J. DiMaggio (eds.): *The New Institutionalism in Organizational Analysis*. Chicago: University of Chicago Press, 1991 pp. 1–38.

Duncan Smith / Smith, Darren P.: *Individualisation versus the geography of 'new' families*. London: London South Bank University. 2006.

Erikson, Erik H: "Identity and the life cycle: Selected papers". *Psychological Issues* 1, 1959, pp. 1–171.

Favell Adrian: "Europe's Identity Problem". *West European Politics* 28 (5), 2005, pp. 1109–1116.

Favell Adrian: *Eurostars and Eurocities: Free movement and mobility in an integrating Europe*. USA, UK, Australia: Blackwell publishing. 2008.

Favell Adrian / Guiraudon, Virginie: The Sociology of the European Union: An Agenda. *European Union Politics* 10(4), 2009, pp. 550–576.

Fligstein, Neil: "Fields, Power, and Social Skill: A Critical Analysis of The New Institutionalisms", 1997. Retrieved 7.3.2012 from: http://www.irle.berkeley.edu/culture/papers/Fligstein3.pdf.

Fligstein, Neil: "Social Skill and the Theory of Fields". *Sociological Theory* 19, 2001, pp. 105–125.

Fligstein Neil: *Euroclash: The EU, European Identity and the Future of Europe*, Oxford, Oxford University Press. 2008.

Fligstein Neil: "Who are the Europeans and how this matter for politics". In Jeffrey T. Checkel, Peter J. Katzenstein (eds.), *European Identity*. Cambridge: Cambridge University Press, 2009, pp. 52–80.

Fligstein Neil / Doug McAdam: *A Theory of Fields*. Oxford: Oxford University Press. 2012.

Fouron, Georges E. / Glick Schiller, Nina: "The generation of identity: Redefining the second generation within a transnational social field". In Hector Cordero-Guzman, Robert Smith, Ramón Grosfoguel (eds.): *Migration, transnationalization and race in changing*. New York. Philadelphia: Temple University Press, 2001, pp. 292–403.

Gargano, Terra: "Reconceptualizing International Student Mobility: The Potential of Transnational Social Fields". *Journal of Studies in International Education* 13 (3), 2009, pp. 331–346.

Geogakakis Didier / Rowel Jay (eds.): *The Field of Eurocracy: Mapping EU Actors and Professionals*. UK: Palgrave MacMillan. 2013.

Georgakakis, Didier: "Civil servant unions and social construction of the European civil service: sociological perspectives on Eurocrats identity", 2006. Retrieved 26.5.2014 from:http://hal.archives-ouvertes.fr/docs/00/12/21/36/PDF/DG-JEI.pdf.

Georgakakis, Didier: "Tensions within Eurocracy? A socio-morphological view". *French Politics* 8, 2010, pp. 116–144.

Georgakakis, Didier / Weisbein, Julien: "From above and from below: A political sociology of European actors". *Comparative European Politics* 8, 2010, pp. 93–109.

Gergen, Kenneth J.: *The Saturated Self: Dilemmas of identity in contemporary life*. New York: Basic Books. 1991.

Giddens, Anthony: *Modernity and Self- Identity*. Cambridge: Polity. 1991.

Giddens, Anthony: In Europe's dark days, what cause for hope? *The Guardian*. 25. 1 2012.

Glick Schiller, Nina: "Transborder Citizenship: An Outcome of Legal Pluralism within Transnational Social Fields". In Franz von Benda-Beckmann, Keebet von Benda-Beckmann (eds.): *Mobile People, Mobile Law: Expanding Legal Relations in a Contracting World.* London, Ashgate, 2005, pp. 27-51.

Glick Schiller, Nina / Basch, Linda / Szanton Blanck, Christina: "From Immigrant to Transmigrant: Theorizing Transnational Migration". *Anthropological Quarterly* 68(1), 1995, pp. 48-63.

Golob Tea: "Slovenian Migrants in Transnational Social Spaces". *Anthropological Notebooks* 15 (3), 2009, pp. 65-77.

Golob Tea / Makarovič, Matej: *Feeling European: transnational participation and identification.* London: Vega Press. 2012.

Golob Tea: "Exploring identifications in the transnational social sphere: the potential of social fields". *Sociologija i prostor* 52 (199), 2014, pp. 123-139.

Guarnizo, Luis E.: "The Rise of Transnational Social Formations: Mexian and Dominican State Responses to Transnational Migration". *Political and Social Theory* 12, 1998, pp. 45-94.

Harvey, David: *The Condition of Postmodernity.* Oxford: Blackwell. 1989.

Hasan, Raquaiya: *Semantic Variation: Meaning in Society and in Sociolinguistics. The Collected Works of Ruqaiya Hasan, Vol 2.* London: Equinox. 2009.

Hooghe, Liesbet: "Images of Europe. How Commissionofficials conceive their institution's role". *Salzburg Papers on European Integration 02-11*, SCEUS Salzburg Centre of European Union Studies/Jean Monnet Centre of Excellence, July 2011. Assesed 14.4.2014, from: http://www.uni-salzburg.at/fileadmin/oracle_file_imports/1941211.PDF.

Ifversen Jan: "Europe and European culture - a Conceptual Analysis". *European Societies* 4, 2002, pp. 1-26.

James, William: *The Principles of Psychology.* London: Macmillan. 1890.

Kearney, Michael: "The Local and the Global: The Anthropology of Globalization and Transnationalism". *Annual Review of Anthropology* 24, 1995, pp. 547-65.

Kellner, Douglas: *Media Culture: Cultural Studies, Identity and Politics Between the Modern and the Postmodern.* London: Routledge. 1995.

Kelly, Phillip / Lusis, Tom: "Migration and the Transnational Habitus: Evidence from Canada and Philippines". *Environment and Planning* 38, 2006, pp. 831-847.

Kostakopoulou Theodora: *Citizenship, Identity, and Immigration in the European Union: Between Past and Future.* Manchester: Manchester University Press. 2001.

Kuhn Theresa: "Individual Transnationalism, Globalisation and Euroscepticism: An Empirical Test of Deutsch's Transactionalist Theory". *European Journal of Political Research* 50 (6), 2011, pp. 811-37.

Lash Scott / Urry, John: *Economies of Signs and Space*. London: TCS. 1994.

Levitt, Peggy / Glick Schiller, Nina: "Conceptualizing simultaneity: Transnational social field perspective". *International Migration Review* 38 (145), 2004, pp. 595–629.

Low, Setha M. / Lawrence-Zúñiga, Denis (eds.): *The Anthropology of Space and Place: Locating Culture*. Malden, Oxford, Carlton and Berlin: Blackwell Publishing. 2003.

Luhmann Niklas: *Social Systems*. Timothy Lenoir and Hons Ulrich Gumbreeht, Stanford University Press. 1995.

Luhmann Niklas: *Die Gesellschaft der Gesellschaft*. Suhrkamp. 1999.

Martin John L.: "What is Field Theory?". *American Journal of Sociology* 109, 2003, pp. 1–49.

Makarovič Matej: "Meje Evrope in globalizacija". *Prispevek na konferenci Kje so meje Evropske unije*, 1. 12. 2008. Retrieved 12.3.2011, from:http://www.ijpucnik.si/media/makarovic,Meje_evropske_unije_in_globalizacija.pdf.

Mastnak, Tomaž: "Mit Evrope in religija demokracije". *Družboslovne razprave* XII (21), 1996, pp. 11–19.

Mastnak, Tomaž: *Evropa: med evolucijo in evtanazijo*. Ljubljana: SH Zavod za založniško dejavnost. 1998.

Mau Steffen / Büttner, Sebastian M.: "Transnationality". In Stefan Immerfall, Göran Therborn (eds,): *Handbook of European Societies. Social Transformations in the 21st Century*. Dodrecht: Springer, 2009, pp. 537–570.

Mau Steffen / Mewes Jan: "Horizontal Europeanisation in Contextual Perspective: What Drives Cross-border Interactions within the European Union?". *European Societies* 14, 2012, pp. 7–34.

Mead, George H.: *Mind, Self, and Society*. Chicago, IL: University of Chicago Press. 1934.

Mishler, William / Detlef, Pollack: "On Culture, Thick and Thin: Toward a Neo-Cultural Synthesis". In Detlef Pollack et. al. (eds.): *Political Culture in Postcommunist Europe: Attitudes in New Democracies*. Hants: Ashgate Publishing Company, 2003, pp. 237–257.

Moallem, Minoo: "Foreigness" and be/longing: Transnationalism and immigrant entrepreneurial experiences". *Comparative Studies of South Asia, Africa and Middle East* XX, 2000, pp. 200–216.

Mokre, Monika: "European Cultural Policies and European Democracy". *The Journal of Arts Management, Law, and Society* 37(1), 2007, pp. 31–47.

Mouzelis, Nicos: "Habitus and Reflexivity: Restructuring Bourdieu's Theory of Practice". *Sociological Research Online* 12(6) 9, 2007.

Mrozowicki, Adam: "The agency of the weak: Ethos, reflexivity and life strategies of Polish workers after the end of state socialism". In Margaret Archer (ed.): *Conversations about Reflexivity*. London: Routledge, 2010, pp. 167–186.

Nora, Pierre: "Foreword." In, Helmut Anheier / Yudhishtir Raj Isar (eds.): *Heritage, Memory and Identity*. New Delhi, Singapore: Sage Publications, 2011, pp. ix–xii.

Peirce, Charles S.: *Collected Papers*. Cambridge: Belnap Press. 1958.

Pioneur Group: "Pioneers of European Integration 'From Below': Mobility and the Emergence of European Identity along National and Foreign Citizens in the EU". Undated. Retrieved 15.2.2014, from:www.obets.ua.es/pioneur/difusion/PioneurExecutiveSummary.pdf.

Porpora, Douglas V. / Shumar, Wesley: "Self talk and self reflection: A view from the US". In Margaret Archer (ed.): *Conversations about Reflexivity*. London: Routledge, 2010, pp. 206–220.

Portes, Alejandro /Guarnizo, Luis E. / Landolt, Patricia: "The Study of Transnationalism: Pitfalls and Promise of an Emergent Research Field". *Ethnic and Racial Studies* 22(2), 1999, pp. 217–237.

Risse, Thomas: "European Institutions and Identity Change. What Have We Learned". In Herrmann, Richard K., Thomas Risse-Kappen, and Marilynn B. Brewer (eds.): *Transnational Identities: Becoming European in the EU U.S.*: Rowman and Littlefield Publishers, Inc, 2004, pp. 247–272.

Risse, Thomas / Maier, Mathias L.: "Europeanization, Collective Identities and Public Discourses". *Final Report, IDNET Thematic Network*. Robert Schuman Centre for Advanced Studies, European University Institute. 2003. Retrieved 15.1.2014, from: http://cordis.europa.eu/documents/documentlibrary/82608121EN6.pdf.

Repič, Jaka: "Ambivalent identities emerging in transnational migrations between Argentina and Slovenia". *Dve domovini* 31, 2010, pp. 121–134.

Riccio, Bruno: "From 'ethnic group' to 'transnational community'? Senegalese migrants' ambivalent experiences and multiple trajectories". *Journal of Ethnic and Migration Studies* 27, 2001, pp. 583–599.

Ritzer, George: *Sociological Theory. Seventh Edition*. New York etc.: McGraw-Hill. 2008.

Rončević, Borut / Makarovič, Matej: "Towards the strategies of modern societies: systems and social processes". *Innovation* 23(3), 2010, pp. 223–239.

Saldana, Johnny: *The Coding Manual for Qualitative Researches*. London: Sage. 2009.

Said, Edward: *Orientalizem: zahodnjaški pogledi na Orient*. Ljubljana: ISH Fakulteta za podiplomski humanistini študij. 1996.

Sassatelli, Monica: "Imagined Europe. The shaping of a European cultural identity through EU cultural policy". *European Journal of Social Theory* 5, 2002, pp. 435–451.

Sassatelli, Monika: "European Identity between Flows and Places: Insights from Emerging European Landscape Policies". *Sociology* 44(1), 2010, pp. 67–83.

Sassen, Saskia: "New frontiers facing urban sociology at the Millennium". *British Journal of Sociology* 15(1), 2002, pp. 143–59.

Sayer, Andrew: "Reflexivity and habitus". In Margaret Archer (ed.): *Conversations about Reflexivity*. London: Routledge, 2010, pp. 108–123.

Savage, Mike / Silva, Elizabeth B.: "Field Analysis in Cultural Sociology". *Cultural Sociology* 7(2), 2013, pp. 111–126.

Shore, Chris: "Whither European Citizenship? Eros and Civilization Revisited". *European Journal of Social Theory* 7 (1), 2004, pp. 27–44.

Seidl, David: "Luhmann's theory of autopoietic social systems". *Munich Business Research paper Nr. 2004-2*. Retrieved 2.2.2014, from:http://www.zfog.bwl.uni-muenchen.de/files/mitarbeiter/paper2004_2.pdf.

Sibeon, Roger: *Rethinking Social Theory*. London: Sage Publications. 2004.

Smith, Michael P.: "Preface". In: Al-Ali N. and K. Koser (eds): *New Approaches to Migration?* London: Routledge, 2002, pp. 2–12.

Sztompka, Piotr: "Civilisational Incompetence: The Trap of Postcommunist Societies". *Zeitschrift fuer Soziologie* 22, 1993, pp. 85–95.

Stråth, Bo: "A European Identity: To the Historical Limits of a Concept". *European Journal of Social Theory* 5, 2002, pp. 387–401.

Tomšič, Matevž: "Evropske vrednote in identiteta - med enotnostjo in različnostjo". *Bogoslovni vestnik* 72, 2012, pp. 627–634.

Tsuda, Takeyuki: "From ethnic affinity to alienation in the global ecumene: The encounter between Japanese and Japanese-Brazilian return migrants". *Diaspora* 101, 2002, pp. 53–91.

Vertovec, Steven: "Transnationalism and identity". *Journal of Ethnic and Migration Studies* 27 (4), 2001, pp. 573–582.

Wacquant, Loïc: "Habitus as Topic and Tool: Reflections on Becoming a Prizefighter". *Qualitative Research in Psychology* 8 (1), 2011, pp. 81–92.

Wertsch, James V. / Billingsley, Doc: "The Role of Narratives in Commemoration: Remembering as Mediated Action". In Helmut Anheier / Yudhishtir Raj Isar (eds.): *Heritage, Memory and Identity*. London, New Delhi, Singapore: Sage Publications, 2011, pp. 25–39.

Wodak, Ruth: "National and Transnational Identities: European and Other Identities Constructed in Interviews with EU Officials". In Herrmann, Richard K., Thomas Risse-Kappen, and Marilynn (eds.): *Transnational Identities: Becoming European in the EU*. U.S.: Rowman and Littlefield Publishers, Inc, 2004, pp. 97–119.

8. Index

A
Adams 10, 11, 18, 23, 83
agency 5, 11–14, 19, 21–23, 28, 29, 46, 77, 78, 83, 89
agential powers 14, 26
Archer 10–14, 19, 26, 46, 61, 73, 83, 85, 89, 90

B
Bhaskar 10
biography 10, 18, 22
Bottero 13, 27, 28, 32, 84
Bourdieu 10–12, 21, 22, 25, 55, 73, 75, 79, 83, 84, 88

C
cognitive maps 25, 26
consciousness 10–14, 24, 32, 41, 45, 50
cultural memory 46–48, 67
cultural policy 42, 90

D
deliberations 9, 10, 13, 14, 19, 24, 26, 48, 77
discourses 35–37, 38, 41, 50, 59, 63, 75, 89
dispositions 11, 13–15, 20, 25–28, 30, 32, 46, 55, 68, 72, 79–81

E
embeddedness 11, 14, 15, 19, 22, 26, 27, 30, 32, 33, 48, 81
emergent entities 10, 19, 47, 79
enablements 9, 13–15, 19, 26, 27, 47, 58, 69, 74, 75, 79–81
ethnographic 7, 51, 57, 58, 69

Europe 35–42, 49, 52, 56, 59–63, 65, 68, 69, 72, 73, 78, 83–88, 90
European identity' 35, 37, 38, 40–44, 45, 51, 63, 68, 84–86, 89, 90
European sphere 45, 78
European structure 49
European Union 35–38, 40–45, 49–51, 55, 57–59, 61, 62, 64–66, 68, 70, 73, 77, 78, 84, 85, 87, 88

F
Favell 43, 49–52, 53, 61, 71, 72, 85
Fligstein 18, 21, 23–25, 27, 29, 31, 45, 49, 50, 52, 56, 68, 71, 78, 81, 86
Fouron 22, 23, 86

G
Giddens 11, 17, 22, 78, 84, 86
Glick-Schiller 22, 23, 28
globalisation 17, 21, 44, 87

H
habitus 10–15, 19, 23, 24, 26, 27, 30, 32, 33, 45, 46, 62, 70, 72, 77, 79–81, 83, 87, 88 90

I
identification 5, 7, 9–12, 17, 19–25, 28–30, 32, 35, 36, 39, 43–46, 48–52, 55–57, 61, 65, 68, 70, 72–75, 77–81, 87
imagined community 36, 44, 46, 48
individualisation 18, 44, 85
inner conversation 14, 15, 79, 81
institutional field 57, 64, 74
instrumental 9, 14, 23, 24, 28–30, 32, 45, 56, 59, 70, 72–74, 77, 80, 81

93

interlocutors 5, 9, 58–61, 63, 64, 67–73, 75, 78
intersubjective 7, 13, 19, 27, 28, 32, 59, 68, 69
interviews 9, 57, 63, 91

L
Levitt 22, 23, 28, 88
life experiences 30, 81
local orders 24
Luhmann 10, 14, 88, 90

M
Mead 12, 17, 88
migrants 28, 51, 83, 87, 89, 90
Morphogenesis 11, 46
Morphostasis 46
Mouzelis 10, 12, 19, 27, 69, 88
multiple identities 28, 44

N
narratives 18, 25, 36, 37, 47, 50, 58, 59, 61–63, 66, 67, 69, 72, 73, 75, 77, 83, 90

O
officials 32, 57, 63–65, 67, 68–70, 91

P
Peirce 12, 89

Q
qualitative study 59

R
reflexivity 10–15, 17, 19, 20, 26–30, 32, 45–48, 61, 70–73, 77, 80, 81, 83, 85, 88–90

resources 13, 14, 18–20, 22, 24–27, 29–32, 35, 50, 52, 53, 55, 57, 60, 61, 63, 65, 66, 69, 70, 73, 74, 80, 81

S
semantics 9, 11, 14, 46–48, 50, 62, 65, 77
social fields 5, 7, 9, 10, 13, 19–25, 27–32, 35, 45, 52, 53, 55, 57, 61, 62, 65, 73, 75, 77, 79, 81, 83, 86, 87
social games 27, 28
social networks 22, 24–28, 43, 52, 65, 66, 73
strategic 7, 9, 23, 30–32, 45, 56, 59, 68, 70, 75, 77, 78, 80
strategically 9, 31, 75
strategies 17, 24, 28–30, 32, 33, 81, 89
structural forces 18, 26, 28, 43, 79
structure 9–13, 15, 17–19, 21, 23, 24, 26, 27, 31–33, 44, 46, 47, 49, 52, 56–58, 64, 69, 74, 75, 77–81, 83, 85

T
thin culture 26, 47
transnational 5, 7, 9, 10, 17, 19–33, 35, 43–46, 48, 50, 53, 55, 57–62, 64, 65, 68, 70–75, 78–81, 83, 84, 86–89, 91
transnational sphere 20, 21, 25, 26, 28, 29, 48–50, 61, 74, 75, 77, 81

V
values 13–15, 18, 25, 32, 35–37, 43, 55, 60, 62, 63, 65, 70, 72, 75, 84

www.ingramcontent.com/pod-product-compliance
Ingram Content Group UK Ltd.
Pitfield, Milton Keynes, MK11 3LW, UK
UKHW021830140426
5217IPUK00021B/1375